MANUAL OF BEL CANTO

MANUAL OF BEL CANTO

By IDA FRANCA

COWARD-McCANN, INC.
NEW YORK

MANUFACTURED IN THE UNITED STATES OF AMERICA

To the most charming Queen Elizabeth II
—in admiration.

I wish to thank Carleton Sprague Smith to whom every reader is indebted for the publication of this manual.

Also, I wish to thank the entire staff of the Music Division of the New York Public Library for its friendliness during my research work. There is no better organized library.

Creative rays of art will brightly shine on you
In days of grief, when life assumes a grayish hue,
If always you will carry high art's holy torch.

And though your skill must root in labor's solid ground
Elysian songs will deep within your soul abound,
If always you will carry high art's holy torch.

Table of Contents

Part I

VOCAL TECHNIQUE

Part II

THE EDUCATION OF THE ARTIST

PART III
THE CASTRATED SINGERS
and Their Role in Bel Canto

APPENDIX
VOICE DEFECTS

TABLE OF FIGURES

TABLE OF GRAPHICAL EXPLANATIONS,
AND MUSICAL EXECUTIONS

PART I

PART II

TABLE OF EXERCISES

Introduction

Singing is a living art, and no one can ever master an art by means of a book exclusively. These pages are only a little manual, written by an artist of the old Italian school, for all those who desire to enter into the spirit of this famous school, which has never betrayed its disciples. Moreover, by means of this handbook I hope to bring an important but often contorted fraction of the old Latin culture nearer to the entire English-speaking world.

In Italy, should a student of singing wish to know if there is any hope of his becoming an artist, he has only to note if and in what manner the wife of the superintendent greets him. If she stops sweeping the stairs when he sings his lines, perhaps he really has a chance of becoming an artist. In Italy, singing is almost the heart and soul of the country; as is painting in France; as is Shakespeare in England; as is baseball in the United States. Since the art of singing is not commonplace in the English-speaking nations, the student cannot rely upon the criticism of his associates. The fact that so many students have asked me: "How can I tell if I am on the right track or making headway?" has inspired me to write this manual. It presents all the famous principles of the old Italian school that produced an endless chain of musicians of vocal perfection.

But this was not the only reason for writing this treatise: I found that not solely the layman and the young voice student, but also many mature musicians completely ignore the real meaning that Bel Canto has in the land of its origin, Italy. I hope the second part of this manual, "The Education of the Artist," will clarify the often encountered yet entirely wrong conception that Bel Canto is, or ever was, a singing method. In this second part the reader will also find Bel Canto's very important musical rules, all their correct musical terms, and the explanation of their graphic signs which not only the vocalists but every coaching pianist, every music teacher, should know—and, alas, rarely do.

Just as the average musician should know more about music, so the B.M. and the B.A., the M.M. and M.A., who are the teachers of music appreciation in the elementary and secondary schools, should have a far better background of musical training and a more thorough knowledge of *music history,* because to them is entrusted the noble mission of planting the seed of longing for real art in the susceptible souls of our youngsters. Throughout the entire manual, these teachers will find much helpful yet often neglected material of musical and general interest. The third part, which is devoted to Bel Canto's castrated enchanters, the famous *musici,* represents something entirely new for nearly all of them. They will learn about a highly artistic period pertaining to our Western culture and will read about mankind's best singers and vocal teachers, of whom they have—at best—only a vague concept. Their lectures will become more interesting; they will be better teachers.

Also, I have incorporated—whenever and wherever it was reasonable—in the text and its footnotes, historical data of importance, as well as minute, concise biographical sketches of the indefatigable giants of the past of whom I have had occasion to speak in this short treatise. Even in first-class encyclopaedias many an error concerning the latter has entered, which, when encountered, I have tried to clarify to the best of my ability. I hope that these clarifications will be welcomed by all who are interested in such studies.

Throughout the treatise the technical and musical terminology belonging to Bel Canto has been adopted, and *many old terms have been translated into English for the first time in history.* Where two or more terms of equal meaning exist, the more customary stands first, the other or others follow, to give the reader full opportunity of becoming acquainted with all of them. For the same reason the correct English translation of the term follows, precedes, or replaces completely the foreign word or words. Whenever I found an English translation of a term to be faulty, the mistake has been rectified. All terms, both technical and musical, have been explained carefully but as simply as possible, so that the novice may also profit from the study of this manual.

Besides explaining in detail the meaning of each term both in writing and graphically, many have been traced through their slow and at times impeded evolution into antiquity. In this I relied on the old writings only. To do so seemed important to me because one cannot depend on the post-Bel Canto literature dealing with the music of ancient Greece; such literature is filled with misinterpretations and absurd distortions, even with terms that never existed. I trust that my retrospects, though simple and short, will add to a full understanding of Bel Canto, how it started, and how and why it matured into the superb musical expression of the Renaissance and the Baroque.

For the many who are interested in artistic lineages, the biographical footnotes have been linked together methodically, so that the artistic roots of most Italian musicians who have been mentioned in this small volume can be traced easily, some into the dawn of Bel Canto.

In addition, I have endeavored at the beginning of the manual to outline in a very short, nontechnical manner the vocal apparatus and its function in singing. I think that every artisan should be familiar with his tools.

I thought it out of place to include voice defects in a treatise on the art of Bel Canto. On the other hand, I was thoroughly cognizant that both the singers and the vocal teachers of our era too often need to be able to discern the springs of the common voice defects, and to learn how these defects may be overcome. Also I wanted our singing youth to be more careful of their God-given voices. To solve the problem I have treated the most frequent voice defects in an appendix.

I hope I have presented my ideas clearly, a feat which is not easy when the subject is art. It is my sincere wish that the perusal of this manual with its graphic explanations, its samples of vocal exercises and its appendix will open the eyes of many who at present are misguided and in error. If I have succeeded in this endeavor, I shall be satisfied.

TO THOSE WHO WISH TO STUDY SINGING

While a beautiful voice is not essential to the study of singing, a "good voice" is; that is to say, a healthy voice in a young and healthy body.

It is also necessary for the student to know what type of voice he possesses. He or she should know whether his or her voice is:

soprano		in the	tenor		in the
mezzo-soprano	}	case of	baritone	}	case of
contralto		women	bass		men

There are many untrained or badly trained sopranos who cannot produce high notes, and there are young, completely untrained contraltos who can easily sing a high c(c^3). Most untrained or badly trained tenors are deficient in their high notes; many even ignore their falsettos, and there are basses with endless falsettos.

Therefore, it is very easy for a student or his friends to make a mistake. Not the range of a voice but its natural color is decisive, and it is exactly the color that often is falsified, especially if the young singer has already studied under an incompetent teacher.

It is advisable for all who purpose serious study to consult on this point an opera singer who has or has had a real career, because this experienced person certainly will not fail to recognize the true type of any voice, in whatever shape it may be presented.

TO SINGERS WHO DREAM OF BECOMING ARTISTS

Anyone who studies an instrument with the intent to achieve complete mastery of it knows very well that he must practice the chosen instrument from six to ten hours a day. In the case of singing, this cannot be done. No professional singer, and positively no student, should exercise his voice more than two hours a day, and those two hours should be broken up into four half-hour periods.[N1]

Nevertheless, just as the serious instrumentalist, the vocalist too must be willing to sacrifice his entire ego to his art, if he aspires to artistry. But students of singing generally are far-off from doing so. They believe themselves to be artists if they possess some high notes or if they can execute a trill. If they have memorized one or two arias, they immediately clamor for an audition; if they know a few more, they feel most positive about giving a successful big concert, and—it sounds incredible—a good many crave to start a singing career, planning to study "afterwards . . . once they have been discovered."

But no one who is not absolute master of vocal as well as singing technique will ever be a virtuoso of the throat. And if after intensive study the gifted student has

---

[N1] Only Negro singers, should they be broad and strong, may exercise their voices three hours a day, and those three hours should be broken up into four forty-five minute periods.

mastered all technique, then he will be a real artist only if always he will be sincere and honest in his art and the severest critic of himself; if he will seek not glory but true art; if he will remain an artist in moments of greatest joy and in moments of deepest gloom. "First my art; then my little self."

A faultless technique may be acquired by study with a good voice teacher, which implies "a vocal virtuoso with a real career *plus* a strongly developed functional hearing." (Functional hearing means hearing that not only perceives all imperfection of sound, but also what causes the imperfection.) Under such expert guidance a gifted aspirant cannot fail to become a vocal virtuoso and a worthy interpreter himself. Yet **the very highest perfection in art cannot be taught;** it can only emerge from within the creative soul of the singer, and it will do so in the course of an intensive career, if the perfectly trained "born-artist" cherishes his art more than success.

TO THE NEGRO SINGER

Frequently the range of the Negro singer—and especially the range of the Negro tenor—can be developed to outdo any white singer's range. Consequently Negro students and singers should read this treatise very carefully, reading it over and over again until they grasp the significance of every single sentence, until they fully understand all the rules of Bel Canto that they may be of real help. Some passages and exercises are written especially for Negro students, and, in addition, they will find a few footnotes marked with an "N" which concern them alone; they should not fail to read them.

Part I

VOCAL TECHNIQUE

§1

Theory of Sound

Sound is a vibratory movement that we perceive with our hearing. Without vibration there is no sound. In order to perceive a sound through hearing, a transmitting medium is necessary, such as air or water.

If the sound wave in the transmitting medium strikes against an obstacle, it is not only deflected but also loses its original quality.

In sound we distinguish pitch, intensity, and timbre (color).

Pitch depends on the frequence of vibrations produced by a sounding body within a given time. The celebrated Helmholtz[1] has demonstrated that the number of vibrations of a cord (wire, string, etc.) in a given time depends on the diameter, the length, and the density of said cord. These vibrations vary in the human voice

from 40.7 (international pitch) for E natural contrabass (E_1) = to

1953 (international pitch) for b natural above high c for soprano (b^3) = per second. (See Table of Registers, p. 15.)

Intensity depends on the nature of the sounding body, on the nature and density of the transmitting medium, and on the distance of the sound receiver from the sounding body.[2] Besides, it is greatly influenced by the "obstacles" that are encountered in the path of the sound wave.

Timbre is the color of sound. There are many theories explaining the cause of timbre. The best known is that of H. L. F. Helmholtz. He has also demonstrated that, in addition to producing primary tones (fundamentals), the body produces secondary tones (overtones) which fuse with the primary tones and thereby modify its timbre. This is known as the theory of harmonics.

May I suggest to all voice teachers—who do not agree with the fundamental rules of Italian voice production which have proved themselves through centuries, and which I am going to treat in this manual—that they read the famous book by the German scientist Helmholtz. After reading the first 120 pages, I feel sure, they will agree.

---

[1] Hermann Ludwig Ferdinand Helmholtz (born in 1821, died in 1894, in Berlin, Germany) was a doctor by profession, but he became immortal as a scientist in the field of art through his book *Die Lehre von den Tonempfindungen als Physiologische Grundlage für die Theorie der Musik*, Brunswick, 1863, tr. by Ellis, 1875—*On the Sensations of Tone as Physiological Basis for the Theory of Music.*

[2] Intensity of sound is in inverse ratio to the square of the distance.

§2

The Vocal Organ

The vocal organ consists of the following: lungs, thoracic cavity, trachea, larynx and epiglottis, pharynx, oral cavity, nasal cavity, and cranial aperture.

The lungs are spongy masses contained in the thorax.

The thorax is formed by the juncture of the dorsal vertebrae in the back, the twelve ribs at the sides, the sternum in front, and the diaphragm below. The diaphragm is a sheet of muscle that separates the abdominal cavity from the thorax.

The trachea (Fig. 1) is a cylindrical fibrous canal that extends from the larynx to the bronchial tubes in the lungs.

The larynx is the producer of the voice. It is a hollow organ with walls formed by various cartilages that are bound together into a cone by means of muscles, membranes, and very elastic ligaments. The latter regulate the movements between the many tiny parts of this delicate organ. That is one of the reasons why no vocal artist should sing or be talkative if he has contracted laryngitis.

The cartilage best known to all is the thyroid cartilage (Fig. 1 and Fig. 2). This cartilage forms the upper anterior portion of the larynx. It consists of two lateral laminae that meet in front at an angle of *circa* 90° in men and of *circa* 120° in women—the Adam's apple (Fig. 2).

Inside the larynx are two pairs of ligamentous muscles. They are the upper or false vocal cords and the lower or true vocal cords (Fig. 1, 3, 4, 5). The true vocal cords are much larger than the false. **The true cords,** the thyro-arytenoid muscles, **produce sound.** The function of the false cords is a protective one.

The limited and variable space between the margins of the true vocal cords is called the glottis (Fig. 3–5). It is the glottis that serves as the passage for the air on its way to and from the lungs.

The epiglottis (Fig. 1) is a yellowish, fibrous cartilage located above and in front of the larynx. This movable lamina of leaflike shape serves to shield the glottis and to separate the pharynx from the larynx during the act of swallowing. The anterior part of this cartilage is attached to the base of the tongue by means of fibrous tissue.

The larynx can also be moved as a single unit, which means that the entire cone can be moved up and down. The upward movement is controlled by the thyrohyoid muscles (Fig. 2), while the downward movement is produced by the sternohyoid muscles (Fig. 2) mostly. For this reason every vocal teacher should be aware that a careful development of these often weak muscles is one of his duties.

Located directly behind the larynx is the esophagus (Fig. 1), the canal that serves to conduct food into the stomach. This canal is very compressible.

The larynx and esophagus open into the pharynx (Fig. 1). This cavity terminates in two branches. One is the mouth, the other the nasal passages.

Between the mouth and the nasal passages we find the soft palate (Fig. 1). It is

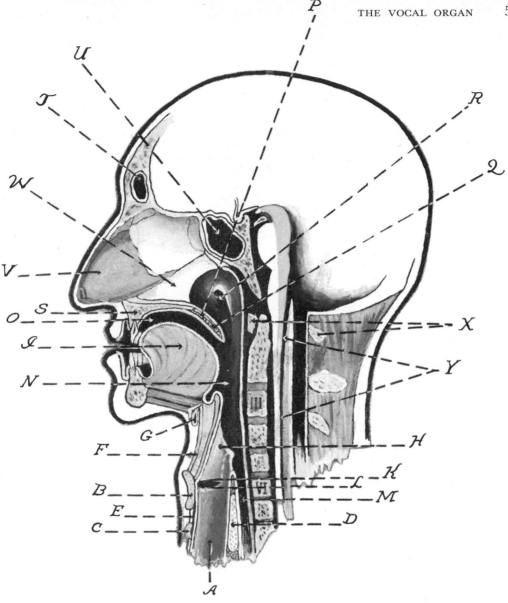

Fig. 1

SAGITTAL SECTION OF HEAD AND THROAT

(a) Trachea
(b) Thyroid cartilage
(c) Arch of cricoid cartilage
(d) Cricoid cartilage
(e) Crico-thyroid membrane
(f) Thyro-hyoid membrane
(g) Hyoid bone
(h) Epiglottis

(i) Tongue
(k) False vocal cord
(l) True vocal cord
(m) Esophagus
(n) Pharynx
(o) Mouth cavity
(p) Soft palate
(q) Uvula

(r) Opening of pharyngo-
tympanic (auditory) tube
(s) Hard palate
(t) Frontal sinus
(u) Sphenoidal sinus
(v) Septal cartilage
(w) Vomer
(x) Atlas
(y) Central canal of spinal cord

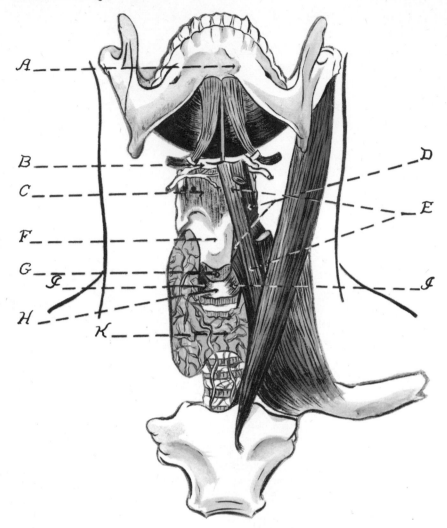

Fig. 2
ANTERIOR MEDIAN LINE OF NECK

(*a*) Lower jawbone
(*b*) Hyoid bone
(*c*) Thyro-hyoid membrane
(*d*) Thyro-hyoid muscle
(*e*) Sterno-hyoid muscle

(*f*) Thyroid cartilage
(*g*) Crico-thyroid membrane
(*h*) Arch of cricoid cartilage
(*i*) Crico-thyroid muscle
(*k*) Thyroid gland

a membrane and the continuation of the bony or hard palate (Fig. 1). In the middle of this membrane runs a fiber which terminates in the uvula (Fig. 1).

This fiber is of utmost importance in singing.[3]

---

[3] It is said of Adelina Patti (1843–1919) that she had a "uvula of gold." Read about her in this Part, footnote 25, p. 23; see also this Part, §9. The Shut Voice, p. 23 and §11.I. Consonants, The famous *morso* . . . , p. 29.

The soft palate ends laterally by means of membranous pillars. Between these tissues the tonsils are located.

And there are, of course, the tongue, the teeth, the lips, the cheeks, the nostrils, etc., etc.

It is well known that the mobility, strength and co-ordination of these organs are of great importance in the various modifications of a sound after it leaves the larynx.

Above the nasal passages are the frontal (Fig. 1), sphenoidal (Fig. 1), ethmoidal sinuses, and the largest sinus contained in the cheek bones, the maxillary antrum. A sound state of the sinuses is most important, because all serve as accessory resonators in a correct voice production—and this not only in singing but also in speaking.

§3

The Voice

The voice is produced by the vocal cords.[4]

But what are the vocal cords and how does it happen that they "sing"?

The vocal cords are two muscles (the thyro-arytenoids) that have the capacity to vibrate after a preparatory effort. This preparatory effort consists in the contraction and in the tension of the vocal cords that have been extended in the act of respiration (compare Fig. 3, 4, 5).

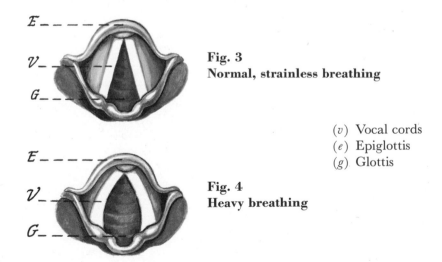

Fig. 3
Normal, strainless breathing

(*v*) Vocal cords
(*e*) Epiglottis
(*g*) Glottis

Fig. 4
Heavy breathing

---

[4] Before the discovery of the laryngoscope, no one knew how. We are indebted to Emanuele Garcia, Jr. for the discovery of the laryngoscope in 1832. Read about him in this Part, §4. footnote 8, second para., p. 10.

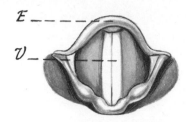

Fig. 5
Preparatory effort

(*v*) Vocal cords
(*e*) Epiglottis

But how can we emit "different" sounds?

The vocal cords are muscles that extend (Fig. 3, 4) and draw near to each other (Fig. 5); that thicken to produce low tones and become thin to produce high tones; that lengthen and shorten according to the tone we want to produce. The air that is emitted by the lungs makes these vocal cords vibrate, and the resulting tone will be high or low, forte or piano . . . just as we had wanted it.

It may be mentioned here that the vocal cords are supplied by a branch of the pneumogastric nerve which at the same time participates in the functions of the vegetative nervous system. Therefore, **the voice** (especially with tenors and sopranos) **suffers greatly from any sexual overindulgence.**

§4

Breathing and Where to Take a Breath

The art in singing lies first of all in the knowledge of correct breathing. (Two centuries ago it was said that singing was the school of breathing.) Therefore, the first condition, and the most essential for good singing, is to be able always to control and dominate both phases of breathing, inhalation and exhalation, and thus to be a "master of breathing."

What must one do to become such a master?

I always say to the tyro: Don't think about it; let me do the thinking. I say this because in worrying about his breathing while singing, the novice loses his breath. But since there are so many harmful methods currently in use, I say to all who wish to sing well:

1) Always (also when not singing) **draw in the part of your abdomen below the navel, as well as the navel itself—AS WELL AS THE NAVEL ITSELF.**

It will take some weeks of intensive concentration and training to reach this most important goal. Besides, strengthen your abdominal muscles by gymnastics or other suitable exercises so that they may never slacken, not even should you feel sick.[5]

---

[5] The abdominal muscles of a well-trained singer are much stronger than those of an average person.

FOR WOMEN: Do not train during the first hours of menstruation, but relax as much as possible.

This will not only help you reach your goal of becoming a good singer, but your body will become more beautiful, your posture will be perfect. You will look taller, healthier, and—that ugly tummy of yours will fade away.

May I mention for those who push and kick with their abdomens as hula dancers do and believe in using the tummy in "singing": **The function of our intestines is to digest the food we eat!** If done well, that is quite a job. Why ask more of them?

2) Put yourself into the physical and spiritual state of one who is going to dive from a great height into the sea, or is training for the championship in running, jumping, and so forth. To repeat this with scholarly precision: keep your shoulder blades (scapulas) in without getting tense, and hold your breath without becoming cramped. I believe that the average inexperienced young person will profit far more from this advice in its first wording, but the teacher should be familiar with both versions.

3) Be happy, radiantly happy.

4) Then, and only then, attack the sound (begin to sing) in the manner that I shall explain in my next chapter. During a phrase never think of the breath, but of the manner of placing each note above the breath.[6]

A singer who keeps his voice above his breath will never be short of breath and will have mastery of his voice—**in singing and in speaking.**

Battistini[7] used to say: "The longer the phrase, the less breath I take, and never more than is necessary to inhale the perfume of a tiny flower. **He who is too full of air** cannot keep his voice above his breath. He **cannot sing.**"

---

[6] See this Part, §6. I. The Registers and Their Union, I have explained . . . , p. 16.

[7] Mattia Battistini of Rome (born February 27, 1857, died November 7, 1928) was the son of an appreciated physician and the most celebrated and cultured modern baritone of the old Italian school. He started to study medicine, but soon decided on singing as his profession. He first studied voice under Eugenio Terziani (1824–1889) of Rome's Santa Cecilia, a pupil of Francesco Saverio Mercadante of the Neapolitan School, who like Bellini had been the disciple of the famous teacher Nicola Zingarelli (1752–1827), the last outstanding master of the typical Neapolitan School (see Part III, footnote 39, p. 108). Later, Battistini studied under Venceslao Persichini (1827–1897), also a teacher at the Santa Cecilia conservatory. (Another famous pupil of Persichini was America's beloved baritone Guiseppe De Luca, 1876–1950). Battistini made his first appearance in Rome at the Argentine Theatre, November, 1878, in Donizetti's *La Favorita*. He was applauded by the audiences of the capital cities of the world and was especially honored and celebrated in Russia, where he sang for the first time in 1892. He was one of the last exponents of Bel Canto and a most eminent interpreter in every sense of the word. He had more than ninety operas in his repertory. Massenet changed *Werther* from tenor to baritone in order to entrust the part to Battistini. In April, 1928, *when seventy-one years old,* he sang in a concert in which he excited the enthusiasm of the public and of the critics in Rome by his clear, youthfully ringing voice, and by the smoothness of his phrasing supported by an endless breath. It was his last bow in front of the censorious aristocracy of Rome. In July he started to be sickly and before the year was over he died.

To the foregoing I may add: "Be happy,"—since I fear that otherwise the novice will hardly be able to inhale the perfume of the little Roman flower as intended by the wise and happily smiling Battistini.

I wish also to quote what has been said, more scientifically but much less simply, by the Garcias, father and son:[8]

"To inhale effortlessly hold the head high, the shoulders in but without tension, the chest free. Then with a slow and regular movement raise the chest itself and make the fontanel of the stomach re-enter. As soon as you begin these two movements, the lungs become more dilated until they are filled with air.

"If the lungs are filled gradually and without shock, they can retain the inhaled air for a long time without discomfort. This inhalation, if done slowly, is called breath (*respiro*). It differs from the other kind of inhalation that is light, instantaneous, and only supplies the lungs with a little air for an immediate momentary need, and that is called half-breath (*mezzo-respiro*).

"In both cases, the passage of air through the throat should not cause the slightest noise, as this spoils the effect of the singing and causes dryness and rigidity in the throat.

"The mechanism of exhalation is the opposite of that of inhalation. It consists of a slow and gradual pressure by the thorax and diaphragm on the inflated lungs.

---

[8] Emanuele Garcia, senior, 1775–1832, was born Emanuele Rodriguez, in Seville, Spain, and died in Paris. He was a celebrated tenor and actor, a composer and an outstanding singing teacher. He was an orphan starting his career as a *puer cantus* [boy singer] when six years old and as a pupil of the Spanish priests Antonio Ripa (1731–1809) and Juan Almarcha (?–?). He made his debut as an opera tenor and composer in Spain, at the age of seventeen years, and made himself a name as a singer and actor in Paris, 1808. While singing in Italy (1811–1816) Garcia studied in Naples with the Roman tenor Giovanni Ansani (1744–1826). Thereafter he became the famous Garcia for whom Rossini in 1816 wrote the part of Almaviva (*The Barber of Seville*). Among his pupils were his daughters Marie (Malibran) and Pauline (Viardot-Garcia), Favelli, the famous Adolphe Nourrit, and his own son, Emanuele Garcia, junior. As with most celebrated artists, various erroneous statements concerning Garcia senior and his teachers have been made which, to the best of my knowledge, I have herein corrected.

Emanuele Garcia, junior, a bass who lived for more than a century, 1805–1906, was born in Madrid and died in Paris. He was his father's pupil, but soon had to abandon the theatre, since he lost his voice because of a bet, as a result of which he tried to prove his vocal power by shouting from one end of Madrid's enormous arena to the betting audience at the arena's other end. Unhappy Garcia then dedicated himself entirely to teaching. In his distress over the loss of his cherished singing career, and ardent to be able to look into the throat and so perhaps to find the reason for his ruined voice, he invented the laryngoscope. He was professor of singing at the Conservatory of Paris and also at the Royal Academy of Music in London. The most celebrated of his star pupils were Jenny Lind, Stockhausen, and Matilde Marchesi. After his father's death Garcia, junior, collected and published his father's manuscripts as *Mémoire sur la voix humaine* (1840) and *Traité complet sur l'art du chant* (1847). Its English translation by Beatrice Garcia is called *Hints on Singing* (1895).

Shocks, panting, the rapid relaxation of the ribs and the instantaneous release of the diaphragm make for sudden expulsion of the breath.

"In fact, the lungs, which are inert and spongy masses, are enveloped in a sort of cone (the thorax), the base of which (the diaphragm) is convex towards the chest. Only one slit of several hairs' breadth (the glottis) located at the apex of the cone serves as passage for the air.

"In order that air may penetrate into the lungs, the ribs must give in laterally and the diaphragm must be lowered. Then only, air fills the lungs. If, in such a state, the ribs fall back and the diaphragm is raised, the lungs, being compressed on all sides like a sponge in one's closed hand, instantly release the air they have inhaled.

"Therefore do not let the ribs fall back nor release the diaphragm except for whatever breath is necessary to feed the sounds.

"The duration of the voice depends on this physical phenomenon."

The foregoing is the scientific explanation of breathing, according to both the Garcias. Part of the valuable contents has been lost in the available English and French editions. Therefore, I have translated the "old wording" because it is the most complete explanation of breathing of which I know, and I believe that not only every teacher, but every person interested in breathing problems of any kind should be familiar with it. It will not help the average novice, because he has as yet no control over his ribs and diaphragm; he will get tense and become cramped.

In order to avoid cramping and to arrive at a favorable result, do not fail to do as I have already advised you at the beginning of this chapter:

1) **Draw in the abdomen below the navel, as well as the navel itself, and keep them thus always, for the rest of your life.**
2) Put yourself in the physical and spiritual state of one who is about to take a high dive into the sea, or is training for the championship in running, jumping, and so forth.
3) Be happy, radiantly happy; please!
4) **Attack and keep the voice above the breath.** This will start you on the road toward your becoming a true and skillful singer.

Where does one take a breath? Where does one take a half-breath?

A full breath, or rather, as old wisdom had it, a calm breath (*la calma del fiato*), should be taken only after the end of the last note of a musical phrase. It should always be taken before a long cadence (*cadenza*), and it should be taken before the finale of such a cadence after the long trill on the fifth.[9] It must never be increased into a big, deep breath.

During a musical phrase, however long it may be, only minimums of air, called half-breaths (*mezzi-fiati*), should be taken, and even they must not be taken *ad libitum* [as one wishes], but always according to the musical and poetic sense.

---

[9] See Part II, Chapter I: A: §5. The Cadences and the Trill of the Finale, p. 76.

§5

Sound Attack

The pupil must next learn to "attack" (initiate) the sound. It is often taught that the sound attack is effected by means of a shock of the glottis. This method of attack is dangerous for many voices, because the shock of the glottis done with force can easily deviate into a shock to the larynx and cause grave vocal alterations. Also no singer will ever be able to produce the flutelike tones (*suoni flautati*) which are so caressing to the ear of the public, if he is used to attack each musical phrase by a shock of the glottis.

The old Italian school teaches that the attack of the sound is completed in two distinct phases: "the preparatory effort" and "the flutelike attack above the breath" (*l'attaco flautato sopra il fiato*).

When a singing tone is to be produced, the vocal cords become tense by contraction and—while drawing close together—take the shape according to the pitch of the note thought of. This physiological act is called the "preparatory effort" or "preparatory act" (page 8 Fig. 5), because it takes place before the beginning (attack) of the sound itself; that is, before the air from the lungs strikes the vocal cords and makes them vibrate. Therefore, the singer should first prepare the sound and then attack it clearly and precisely without shock.

What should be done to achieve this goal?

One should take the sound from without and carry it into the focus of the resonances, which is located in the head, then attack it at the very focus. The idea of taking the sound from without, carrying it into the focus of the resonances, and attacking it there and **never in the throat** seems strange, yes, maybe absurd, but in reality it will gradually enable the beginner to liberate his entire "should-be-flexible" vocal apparatus from all rigidity. The vocal cords then have time to contract properly, and the air which has been compressed in the lungs makes the vocal cords vibrate without shock and without any trace of effort. This flutelike method of attack (*modo flautato* or *a flauto*) will not allow the slightest escape of breath without its serving in the production of sound.

Any voice that allows air to escape which is not completely utilized in voice production is defective due to some physical defect, such as nodules, or to poor breath control. If the first cause is responsible, one should go to a doctor; if the second, the voice teacher should be able to help.[10]

Since the sound attack should always be preceded by the preparatory act, and since every note should first be thought of and then sung—even in the fastest agility—the expression "putting a piece into the throat" will then be understood.

---

[10] Voice teachers should now insert the reading of the Appendix, §3. The Veiled Voice, p. 131.

Every good school therefore preaches that one should never sing any composition before having grasped it by ear, which means with the mind.

It is, of course, to be understood that not only the artist but the advanced student as well does not "take the sounds from without" to carry them into the resonances. He "lives in the resonances" (*dans le masque*) both in singing and in speaking— always. He has no need of this imaginary device of taking the sounds from without in order to relax the vocal organ and to place the voice above the breath. That must be a part of himself long before the study of his repertoire can be started with real artistic results. Neither will he have to think of the notes (preparatory act) before singing them. Nevertheless, he will attack any musical phrase in a sweet, flutelike manner because doing so has become second nature to him.

Once again: what I have just explained is not intended for artists who know how to sing; it is merely to help the tyro reach a most important goal: **to free his entire vocal apparatus of all tension.**

I would like to add at this point that such a sound attack will also be the first step for any speaker with throat troubles for acquiring a full and pleasant speaking voice which never will fatigue the throat—the longing of many men and women who have to deal with the public.

FOR VOICE TEACHERS: Never explain to a student the exact location of the focus of his resonances; you would be sure to handicap him greatly if you did this. The novice has to "experience" first his head resonances and consequently their focus before there should be any talk about the focus. Most students start doing so after a few lessons, if you, the teacher, have a functional hearing to guide them. Just **insist that the tyro take smilingly each note from without, somehow from somewhere up in front of him, carrying it mentally down into his head**—not into his throat or mouth; **that he sing for an imaginary audience sitting somewhere below and behind him, not in front of him; that he never slacken the part of his abdomen under the umbilicus.** Be most vigilant and insistant; stop him each time he attacks wrongly with a shock of the glottis, wants to push, wants to sing with a tremolo, raises his shoulders for breathing, and/or gasps air like a fish out of water. Also, right away from the first lesson train him to stand straight on both his feet with the entire part of his body above the umbilicus neither rigid nor lolling but supple, with his scapulas kept in with ease and with arms plus hands that neither gesticulate nor cramp, but which fall loosely to his sides. If the beginner finds it too strenuous to keep the abdomen below the navel drawn in, because his or her abdominal muscles are weak, try to let this student stand with his feet closed; it may help him to acquire the badly needed correct posture. But, dear fellow teacher, be patient. It is on your time and not on the time the tyro pays for that he should rest whenever he tires, gets tense, or feels dizzy; the latter will occur as soon as his head resonances, not used before in phonation, start responding. Be encouraging when his cheeks tremble, and, for a few weeks, divide each lesson for this pupil into two or three brief teaching periods. Soon such quiver should disappear, never to frighten the student again. In short, be very kind to the novice who in good faith tries to adjust his ego to something entirely new and extraneous to him. You know that it is difficult to grasp. Soon you will hear his voice starting to focus, and he will be talking about the different sensations he has in his head. Dear fellow teacher with a functional hearing, let him have his say; do not upset him by contradicting if his "discoveries" are not exact; it suffices that he starts to be conscious of his head resonances. He will change his ideas over and over again until you will have completely focused the voice. Then, and only then, can he fully understand. But if you are not sensitive to your own focus, or worse, if you, the teacher, even are not sure where the famous "focus of the resonances" is located, then you will have a hard time teaching voice production with good results.

§6

Emission and Quality of the Voice

While the quality of the voice is a gift from God, this quality often lies hidden in the student, and it is the duty of the teacher to discover it. The majority of uncultivated voices are defective, and it is the business of the teacher to eliminate the defects and to "clean the voice" in order to bring out its beauty.

How can this be attained?

It can be attained by unifying the registers and taking care of the timbre (color) of the voice.

I.   THE REGISTERS AND THEIR UNION

By register we mean a group of sounds that are akin. We distinguish the following: a) chest register, b) falsetto or mixed register, c) head register.

Since this is only a manual, I shall not give the physiological explanation of the registers but will confine myself to giving, in the following Table of Registers, three complete pictures of the registers according to the old Italian school.

From these pictures the reader will see that a great number of notes can be produced in two registers, whence arises the possibility of unifying the registers.

From these pictures of female and male voices, one can also see that by and large, members of the Negro race have a wider voice range than people of the white or yellow race. This is one of the reasons why Negro voices are often especially rich, flexible and beautiful. With proper study some Negroes could become leading singers of the future.[N2]

The unifying of these registers (three for women, two for men, three for Negro tenorinos [light tenors]) is the duty of the teacher. All voices are more or less weak or defective in one of the registers. It is the duty of the teacher to develop his pupil's

---

[N2] See this §. II. The Timbre of the Voice, footnote N4, p. 21.

Fig. 6
TABLE OF REGISTERS*

COMPLETE PICTURE OF FEMALE VOICES IN THEIR THREE REGISTERS

COMPLETE PICTURE OF MALE VOICES IN THEIR TWO REGISTERS

COMPLETE PICTURE OF NEGRO MALE VOICES IN THEIR THREE REGISTERS

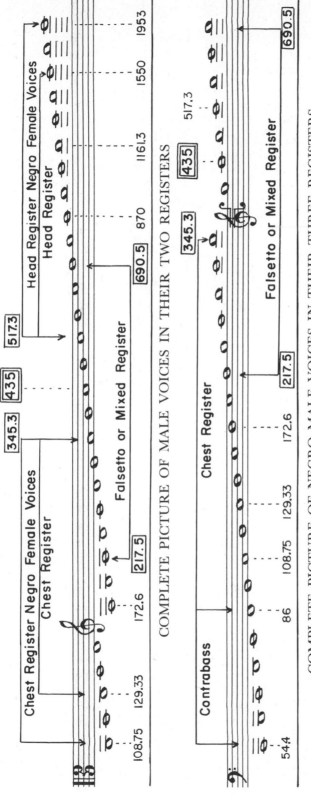

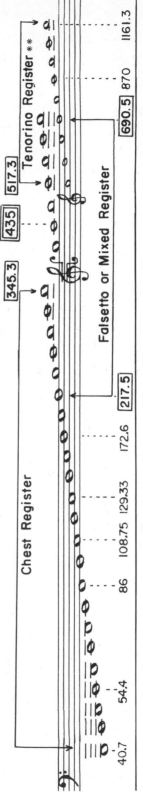

* All indications as to the number of vibrations are those in use on our well-tempered piano, international pitch, $a^1 = 435$ (America's concert pitch, $a^1 = 440$).

** This register corresponds, as is obvious, to the head register of female voices. Through this head voice, cultured and refined to perfection, the famous castrated singers of two centuries ago won immortality.

weaker register with appropriate exercises, and to place the entire voice in such a manner, as to give the listener the impression that the singer has no "change of registers." Even the artist himself will deny the very existence of the registers. Personally, I have no registers in my voice. I attack and sing ♯ in the same manner as ♮

Every voice that throughout its entire range is both placed above the breath (shut-in in the head) and firmly anchored in the chest is perfectly balanced and, therefore, will give the most critical audience as well as the performing artist the sensation of a single register.

I have explained in the preceding chapter (§5) how to attack "above the breath" and to free the vocal apparatus from all tension. Now to place the entire voice surely above the breath and to keep the throat open as well as in complete relation with the resonances, I advise all young vocal students (basses, baritones, tenors, contraltos, mezzo-sopranos, and sopranos of all kinds) to hold fast to the idea of taking all sounds from without and of singing in the focus of the resonances. Also, the student should think of the listeners as being behind him and not in front of him, and his teacher should make him feel at ease and happy.

A beginner should not study sustained notes[11] but articulate the voice from high to low. He should never try to carry the chest voice into the head register, but should start using the $\begin{cases} \text{head voice for women} \\ \text{falsetto voice for men} \end{cases}$ for the notes belonging to the chest register, while taking care to avoid any shock of the glottis. This may be very difficult in the beginning, and much patience may be needed, but every voice can and should learn to do so.

To articulate a student's voice in the beginning from "high to low" and not from "low to high" is a golden rule already established and fought for by Aristotle *circa* 2300 years ago; it has been applied throughout the entire Bel Canto era by teachers who made mankind's greatest vocal artists and were virtuosos themselves—by Porpora, Bernacchi, Tosi, Senesino, and so forth.[12] No modern teacher should flatter himself that he knows better than these men.

Also one must not drag the note that one is singing over to the following note, and so forth, because the result would be a wail and never a legato. Instead, the

---

[11] See Part II, Chapter I: A: §2. VI. Sustained Notes, p. 63.

[12] For a correct understanding of the "era" of Bel Canto see Part II, Chaper I: A: §1. Explanation of the Expression "Bel Canto," p. 37.

For Porpora see Part II, footnote 25, second para., p. 58.

For Bernacchi see Part III, The *Musici,* Bernacchi, p. 103.

For Tosi see Part III, The *Musici,* Tosi, p. 121.

For Senesino and his statement concerning this rule see Part III, the *Musici,* Senesino (Tenducci), p. 120.

student should place mentally each successive note—taken from without—on top of the preceding, on top of the one he is just singing. He should do this until the voice in all its registers becomes unified and only one register can be heard (*voix mixte* = mixed voice). For a complete understanding insert now the reading of the § dealing with legato singing.[13]

I teach my students in the following manner:

I show the girls how to attack on the first or second note of their head register, and I choose the more limpid one. I make them use this head voice for the notes of the falsetto register until head and falsetto voice blend (mix). I make them use this mixed head and falsetto voice also for the first chest sounds until it fuses with them.

Not uncommonly it is necessary to correct a female voice that has never made use of the sweetness of the mixed voice, but has for years forced the chest voice to produce all sounds belonging to the delicate and sensitive falsetto and head registers. Consequently, when the singer has reached the thirties, difficulty with the high notes is encountered. For such a voice I choose the sound of the head register that has remained most natural, and from this note the difficult task of placing that voice above the breath begins.

I show the men—even the Negro tenorinos[N3]—how to attack on the best note of their falsetto or mixed register, and I work with them a fifth below in the same manner as I work with my girls. I limit their working range in the beginning to an octave, until the falsetto voice easily blends into the chest voice.

There are many men, even tenors, who ignore completely the existence of their own falsetto voice. They use exclusively the chest voice; consequently, their tones are only fundamentals, and all overtones are missing (see p. 3). The result is that they not only have difficulty with their high notes, but they also cannot flex their voices. They shout, they do not "sing." They will become excellent singers if they have the patience to train under the careful guidance of a very conscientious voice teacher who will insist that they stop cultivating the crude chest voice. Such a male singer must first learn to sing pianissimo on a few notes of his falsetto register until he has acquired the knack of using his inborn but neglected falsetto voice. Sometimes, but not always, trying to make the pupil imitate the teacher's shut voice[14] will be helpful. Of course, only **after** such training can one begin the task of unifying and developing this voice into a mixed voice, as in the above manner.

I work tirelessly in these more or less limited extensions already treated, and never lose my patience. In order not to bore the novice, and *to educate him musically while I am placing his voice* faultlessly above the breath, I change and rechange the simple

[13] See Part II, Chapter I: A: §2. The Beginning of the Study of Bel Canto and Legato Singing, p. 38.

[N3] Be careful, Negro light tenors, your tenorino register definitely has to be developed. You will be able to find it, only after your falsetto register has been perfectly united with your chest register in the way I am explaining in this manual.

[14] See this Part, §9. The Shut Voice, p. 23.

exercises, as elaborated in Part II of my treatise, until I have succeeded in molding his voice; and it is in this early period of vocal instruction that I start training the student to vocalize also *a cappella* [unaccompanied] without singing off pitch and/or distorting the rhythm. Said constancy and patience in the vocal as well as musical education have most important bearing upon the whole future of the pupil.

When the voice begins to blend in the registers, I develop more and more the head register in women, and the falsetto register in men. I work gradually upward, and—maintaining a proper balance—I also work more and more downward into the chest register, because **high and low tones must be developed at the same time.** Thus the voice will mature into brilliance, body, and flexibility. I always work with the greatest caution, avoiding any possible strain on the vocal apparatus; I invite the student to sit and rest whenever he feels dizzy and never permit any student to sing sustained notes in this period of training. I flex and move the voice until the registers are perfectly united, until the entire range of the voice is placed securely above the breath (*sopra il fiato*) in the focus of the resonances (shut-in in the head, *dans le masque*), is always free in the throat, and is firmly anchored in the chest.

Too often nowadays this principle of the old Italian school that had its roots in the dogmas of Aristotle is neglected. Therefore, I wish to repeat most clearly this *sine qua non* of singing, because on it rest all vocal virtuosities that outlast youth: **Every note of the entire range of any voice in all its manifold shadings, kinetics and dynamics must always be**

1. **mentally produced and kept above the breath in the focus of the resonances,**
2. **completely free in the throat,**
3. **firmly anchored in the chest.**

Consequently the highest sounds of any voice always, even on pianissimo, must be anchored in the chest; the lowest sounds of any voice always, even on forte, must be shut-in in the head.

And if one bright day my pupil says to me: "It's strange, but I have the feeling of being above my own voice; *I feel so free*"; or if he says to me: "I believe I don't need any breath; *I feel light as a feather;* I never thought singing to be so easy"; then I have not worked in vain; then he or she is on the right road to becoming an artist.

I assume that many a reader would now like to ask why one cannot succeed in unifying the registers by starting from the chest tones, blending the voice by working upward. I reply: Within the men's chest register, and within the women's chest and falsetto registers, there are many ways of singing. Try them all! The notes of the women's head register and those of the men's falsetto register can be sung "with ease" and beauty in one manner only. It is, therefore, necessary to start training a voice in the manner most suited to the { head register for women / falsetto register for men } and adopt and use this one way throughout all the registers.

Then the female voice in its high register will never sound like the shrill whistle of a locomotive,[15] nor will the male voice ever break ("crack") while singing forte on a high note. Their voices will always be unified, plastic, and agile, and **these artists will know only a single register.** In some rare cases such a "mixed voice" may be a little thin in the first few years.[16] Yet with the passing years it will become more and more robust in the entire range, without losing its great flexibility.

The union of the women's head register with that of the falsetto is not difficult, but the union of the falsetto register with the chest register is hard work for women as well as for men.

If these registers (falsetto and chest register) are not perfectly united, after a few years the male voices lose their high notes, while the female voices, besides losing their top notes, develop the unfortunate break ("hole") in the center of the voice. It is the sad beginning of an artist's decadence.

FOR WOMEN: From all that I have said, you may gather that the female voice is more delicate than the male voice and that the weak spot for women is the falsetto register. It is there that the voice soon feels the abuse of both high and low notes, and it is in this range that the decadence of female voices originates.[17] These are the notes that all women singers must take care of every morning during their entire career, whether it be during idle periods, periods of study, or while passing from success to success.

FOR NEGRO WOMEN: More than all other female singers, you must take care of your falsetto register. This register, as I have demonstrated in my "Complete Picture of Female Voices in Their Three Registers" (see p. 15), is the only one which is equal in range to all other female voices. Unfortunately, however, some of you use it merely as a loose bridge between your flexible head register and your—sometimes—huge chest register. I hope that you have grasped by now that the falsetto register must never degenerate into such a "bridge." Be very careful in the selection of your voice teacher. Be diligent and patient, and you surely will surpass your white sister!

FOR NEGRO TENORINOS: Turn now to Part III and read about the famous castrated singers. A few of you should be able to step into their paths and fill the emptiness that they left—and this without the sacrifice of your virility. If you will train to sing in the mixed voice only, and if you will use this mixed voice in the manner that you find treated throughout this manual, high notes belonging to the tenorino register (which, as you know by now, corresponds to the female head register) will emerge without any strain, as though by themselves. They will do so slowly

---

[15] See Appendix, §2.d) Hooting Voice, p. 131.

[16] During the first years of his career, Caruso was called the "windy tenor" (*tenore vento*), and what a colossus he later turned out to be!

[17]  Herein originates not only the famous break, but it is here, always in the case of women, that the sensitive ear hears if the vocal cords are irritated. See Appendix, §3. The Veiled Voice, p. 131.

but surely; then, step by step, slowly but surely, your voice in its new, enormous range will become a powerful caress. "If"—if you are just as gifted and will be just as patient and diligent as the poor Italian castrated boys used to be, you will surpass any tenorino of any race because of your three registers, and also quite a few of our female stars because of the masculine capacity of your lungs.

FOR VOICE TEACHERS: May I advise you to reread not only this most important § dealing with the registers and their union, but to study the Table of Registers until you fully understand the deep reason why a perfect unifying of the falsetto or mixed register with the chest register is of the utmost importance in the career of your pupils, be they men or women. Besides, by checking carefully the number of vibrations you will see that the tenor clef we use today is just an octave lower than the treble clef. A tenor's high a = (♪435) corresponds to (435) and not to (870) as some teachers believe. (It is an a^1—not an a^2.) Do not train a student constantly to vibrations twice as frequent as those of his pitch. You harm his voice. He will squeeze and force his sounds.

FOR VOICE TEACHERS WHO ARE MY FORMER PUPILS: Let me remind you that it was in this early period of vocal instruction "after" I had awakened the focus of your resonances, and you had already become sensible to it, and while I was molding and unifying the registers of your voice, that I started teaching you the famous PLAY OF THE DIAPHRAGM. Let me also remind you for the sake of your pupils that this was done without your awareness of my intentions and that I never mentioned the diaphragm while I was teaching you to use it, for fear that you might start cramping—until suddenly you felt it playing as by itself. Remember how I demonstrated over and over again, until you succeeded in inhaling and exhaling most rapidly, yet noiselessly, with ribs that never fell back, with the lower jaw loose in its sockets, and with the lips completely shut. Remember that such half-breaths never were permitted to touch even lightly the nasal passages. I did not discuss everything I showed you and asked you to do, and, to a few of you, I had to refuse vocal philosophy; but I steered each one of you out of his tenseness and stiffness or lack of vitality, or plain sloth. Assiduously, in every single lesson, I both innervated and loosened you until slowly you became the full master of your breath. You will have to do the same, if you wish to work with real success.

II.   THE TIMBRE OF THE VOICE (COLOR)

By the expression "timbre of the voice" we mean the color of the voice. This color has an individual or personal quality that depends on the formation of the singing apparatus and resonances just as the physiognomy of every being depends on the shape of his head and face. This color of the voice is as variable as a facial expression, changing from a smile to tears.

Just as we have long and round faces, so we have voices of varying natural colors:

white, dark, and yellow. The most beautiful are the "naturally" dark voices.[N4] But we can also change the personal color of the voice to a brighter or a darker shade.[18]

The old Italian school teaches that a well timbred (colored) voice will be produced if the student learns to sing in rounded and bright tones (*sul chiaro rotondo*).

And how is that possible?

If one attacks in the manner already explained,[19] above the breath in the focus of the resonances, on the vowel *a*,[20] the voice will be bright but round. If the reader is Italian, I say to him: "Take care not to make an overopened *a* (*a spalancato*); the *a* must be free in the throat *plus* shut-in in the head."[21] To my English-speaking readers—and it is for them that I have written this manual[22]—I would say: "Take care that the *a* be clear as in the English words 'father, arm.' Be careful that this *a* sound remains clear throughout the exercise and that it does not change into an *a* such as the one in 'has, hand' or as the one in 'call, war.'"

The voice timbred in such a manner will penetrate because it is bright, and will be sweet because it is round. These are two essential qualities for singing in large concert halls or theaters and becoming a favorite of the public.

Nowadays many defective timbres are not cured properly. Worse, some even are taught by teachers who do not know better; world-wide vocal decadence is the result. To discuss the defective timbres, with all their destructive consequences, in the body of a treatise on Bel Canto would be out of place, but the reader will find them treated in the appendix of this manual.

§7

Sound Detachment

Few teachers pay any attention to the detachment of sound. It is, however, most important.

A singer who attacks and sings well, but releases the last note of a phrase badly, ruins his own work and tires easily.

How does one release the sound correctly?

[N4] Most Negro voices are naturally dark; this is one of the reasons for the beauty of these voices. See also this §, I. The Registers and Their Union, p. 14.

[18] See Part II, Chapter II: §3. The Application of Various Timbres, p. 87; see also Appendix, §2. d) Hooting Voice, p. 131 and e) Shrill Voice, p. 131.

[19] See this Part, §5. Sound Attack, p. 12.

[20] See this Part, §10. The Study of the Vowels and Diphthongs and Their Application to English Singing, p. 25.

[21] See Appendix, §2. e) Shrill Voice, p. 131.

[22] The Italians, especially the Southern, almost always speak with an open throat. Therefore it is easier for them to acquire the skill of placing the voice above the breath, and teaching them is a much more simple matter.

The answer is: By cutting off the sound, but retaining the breath.

Lest the reader may not understand this, I shall try to explain it graphically.

In this manner, the voice will end a phrase cleanly and avoid the trailing lament (*coda lamentosa*) that is often heard when a singer (he cannot be called an artist) is not completely the master of his breath.

§8
The Mouth and Lips in Singing

a) **THE MOUTH:** Many believe that for singing well one has to open the mouth exaggeratedly. This is a harmful mistake. If a voice is delicate, it might be damaged; if it is robust, its owner will mature into a noisemaker not a singer. Instead, the lower jaw has to be trained to be extremely mobile in its sockets. Such training should be done cautiously, else some beginner might dislocate his lower jaw or damage the ligaments of his sockets.

b) **THE LIPS:** I have not yet spoken of the manner of lip formation. I have advised attacking and singing while happy. The happy man smiles, smiles in a supple and free manner. Since I want every vocal student to sing with an easy, natural smile and not with a tense grin, I say "Be happy!"[23]

May such a serene attitude become second nature to him—not only while he sings but always; may it grow to be part of his young ego, because it will be of great help to him and to his career as an artist.

FOR VOICE TEACHERS: If a student has difficulty in singing while smiling happily, and constantly opens his mouth exaggeratedly or squeezes his jaws rigidly, he should sing every exercise first while holding a clean, small cork between his front teeth, so that the distance between the incisors is a half to three-quarters of an inch. Then the exercise should be repeated without the cork. It will help, **but only** if you teach him correctly. Besides, every future singer or public speaker should be trained in the reading and reciting of poetry with an open and free throat, and with his voice above his breath as previously elaborated. Also in this endeavor the holding of the

---

[23] See this Part, §4. Breathing and Where to Take a Breath, p. 8 and this Part, §6. I. The Registers and Their Union, p. 16.

small cork between the front teeth while reading or reciting will prove of real help if used in moderation, and if taught correctly. Such daily training for ten minutes or so will make the student's speech clear and pleasing, his phrasing more refined, and, above all, will strengthen and prepare his entire vocal apparatus for the difficult task of enunciating clearly while singing.

§9
The Shut Voice (Voce Chiusa)

The contraction and movements of the soft palate are most important in voice emission. I omit physiological explanations in this manual, stating only that the movements of the soft palate are inverse to those of the larynx.

The greater the elasticity, strength, and control by the singer of his soft palate that terminates in the uvula,[24] the greater will be the mastery of his voice. It was said of Patti that she had a "uvula of gold."[25]

To lead the vocal student toward the maximum development of his or her talent, one should start with the study of the *voce chiusa* [shut voice] as soon as possible, and take the utmost care that the beginner does not shut the mouth and hum.

Both the well-known hum and Bel Canto's shut voice are sung without articulating. **The resonator for the hum is the anterior cavity of the mouth; for the shut voice it is the entire skull.** To sing a tune without articulation in the way Moreschi or Battistini[26] used to do cannot be achieved by humming, but only by using the shut voice.

I teach my pupils to attack, sing, and cut off a shut sound in the same way as when vocalizing: that is, above the breath **in the focus of the resonances,** free in the throat, and firmly anchored in the chest. To avoid any nasalization, I see to it that they do so with wide-open nasal passages and, if necessary, help them to strengthen the nasal muscles.[27] To strengthen the soft palate I insist that every shut

---

[24] See this Part, §2. The Vocal Organ, p. 4.

[25] Adelina Patti (born in Madrid, Feb. 19, 1843, died in her castle in Wales, Nov. 27, 1919) was one of the greatest virtuosi of the throat. She was the daughter of Salvatore Patti, a good tenor, and of Caterina Chiesa, who also was a professional singer with a well-trained voice. When only four years of age Adelina trilled like a bird; when six years of age she faultlessly imitated the most difficult vocal virtuosities of Jenny Lind (1820–1887) and other stars. Little Adelina got her excellent fundamental vocal and musical education from her parents. She made her American concert debut when only twelve years of age, and her opera debut at the age of sixteen. Read about her life in her book *My Reminiscenses* (1909); it will be enjoyable.

[26] For Moreschi see Part III, The *Musici,* Moreschi, p. 116. For Battistini see this Part, footnote 7, p. 9.

[27] See Appendix, §2.a) Nasal Voice, Weak nasal muscles, p. 129.

sound be sung by a beginner with the mouth opened as while singing a clear *a* and with a supple smile on the lips.

Once they understand how to shut their voice in the manner explained above, I teach them to shut, open (first to an *a*, as in the words "father, arm," but gradually to all other vowels),[28] and re-shut on one and the same breath every note of their range without the slightest interruption, disturbance (such as clicking) or any other alteration (such as nasalization). Then I include the shut sound in all exercises—even those on trills. When they are more advanced, I teach them first to sing each piece in a faultless shut voice, then, "afterwards," to sing the piece with its words, and to study persistently every difficult passage in the shut voice until the difficulty is overcome. No difficult or new passage should ever be studied in an undertone (*sotto voce*), because the *sotto voce* is a soundless, incomplete voice that does not rest above the breath. A perfect shut voice is a most complete voice, and is the students' as well as the mature artists' best friend. For this reason, all advanced students should start their training every morning with the shut voice.

A note that cannot be sung on one and the same breath in a shut as well as in a normal, open voice, and this without the slightest interruption, disturbance or any other alteration, is not completely dominated, because it is not shut-in in the head while anchored in the chest; consequently this note is not perfect.

We all have one or, if we are tired, even two high notes at the limit of our vocal compass that we can produce, but that we are not capable of singing on one and the same breath in the "shut-open-shut" manner without any slightest alteration. **These one or two notes are not perfect and therefore are not for the public.**

It is extremely difficult to achieve absolute mastery of the soft palate and uvula. But with patience and work every singer can accomplish it. Everything that is worth doing is worth taking the trouble to do well, since he who is the absolute master of his uvula can do whatever he pleases with his voice. He can render it bright or dark, happy or sad, cruel or pleading; and he can do so without the slightest effort.

Furthermore, the daily use of the shut voice forms a sure control for the mature artist himself, and, above all, maintains the youthful color of his voice as long as he lives.

For Negro Students: Take care that the shut voice does not become nasal. You are susceptible to it. This happens for manifold physiological reasons which cannot be explained in a handbook on Bel Canto. If this happens to you, be sure to strengthen your nasal muscles,[N5] and think of swallowing your own sound while singing. But, please, keep smiling—please, feel happy!

For Voice Teachers: The shut voice, this vocal ability that slowly but surely leads to the sovereign mastery of the voice, can only be learned through imitation and never through explanation. If you do not possess a perfect *voce chiusa* you can-

---

[28] See this Part, §6. II. The Timbre of the Voice, p. 21; see also this Part, §10. The Study of the Vowels and Diphthongs and Their Application to English Singing, p. 26.

[N5] See Appendix, §2.a) Nasal Voice, Weak nasal muscles, p. 129.

not teach it. Should you try, you may damage your trusting pupils' vocal apparatus. Instead, you could go to learn this vocal ability from some artist of the real old Italian school of vocal virtuosity. A few of the old guard are still with us, and I have raised and still am raising some good substitutes to carry on. It should not take long to learn from such a person, and it surely is worth the trouble.

§10

The Study of the Vowels and Diphthongs and Their Application to English Singing

The study of vocalization should begin in the early period of teaching, after the first obstacles have been overcome, when the student knows how to sing within the middle range without losing the right track, and without changing from the *a* of "hard" to that of "have" or to that of "was."

At the same time the study of the semitones[29] and of the legato agility[30] should commence. But the study of the trills[31] and of the sustained tones[32] should not be attempted till later, nor that of any non-legato agility.[33]

From this it can be seen that a sensible method of study will never be monotonous. A true teacher of the old Italian school will teach his pupil to vocalize while taking the utmost care that the emission should become faultless. At the same time such a teacher will introduce his pupil to the technique of Bel Canto[34] within the limit of the vocal extension of the moment, which will increase without any effort when guided correctly.

Let us return to the vowels. We distinguish seven *pure* vowels:

1) *i* (see, feel; in, ill)
2) *é* (there, care) closed *e* (*e chiuso*)
3) *è* (send, Lent; pen, pet) open *e* (*e aperto*)
4) *a* (father, arm) the basis of the Italian voice emission
5) *ó* (note, oak) closed *o* (*o chiuso*); in America the *o chiuso* is often quite pure; in England, for the most part, it only starts as a pure vowel and glides to an impure vowel resembling *oo* (7)

---

[29] See Part II, Chapter I: A: §2. II. The Semitones and the Chromatic Scales, p. 41.

[30] See Part II, Chapter I: A: §2. The Beginning of the Study of Bel Canto and Legato Singing, p. 38.

[31] See Part II, Chapter I: A: §2.V.a) Trills, p. 56.

[32] See Part II, Chapter I: A: §2.VI. Sustained Notes, p. 63.

[33] See Part II, Chapter I: A: §3. Non-Legato Singing, p. 68.

[34] See Part II, Chapter I: A: The Technique of Bel Canto, p. 37.

6) *ò* (moral, sorry; Goth, doff) open *o* (*o aperto*); in America the open *o* (*o aperto*) is much less heard than in England—it is either broadened (doll, dollar) or more or less darkened (God, song)

7) *u = oo* (blue, lose; book, look)

The vowel *a*(4) is the one most suitable for attaining a free and open throat. Therefore, all the exercises should be executed on *a*(4), not only by beginners but also by the more advanced. However, since all the vowels are used in singing, it is wise to practice them also at an early stage.

The *é*(2) and the *ò*(6) vowels are difficult for most voice students of the English-speaking nations. Both the teacher and the student will have to be on guard that the *é*(2) vowel does not shift during an exercise into an *i*(1); often the teacher will have to show over and over again the *é*(2) vowel to a beginner who cannot produce the pure *é*(2) but uses instead some diphthong he is accustomed to. The *ò*(6), the Italian much used *o aperto*, is a real headache not only to those whose native tongue is English, but also to those whose mother tongue is any other Germanic language. Nearly all—not only beginners—sing an *ó*(5) when the word asks for an *ò*(6). An early command of both *ó*(5) and *ò*(6) in vocalization will safeguard from such mispronounciation in the later text singing.

The vowels *i*(1) and *u = oo*(7) are not suitable for developing an open throat. The *i*(1) raises the larynx to the very top, while the *u = oo*(7) sends the larynx down completely. It will, therefore, be more difficult to render these vowels in a loose and free manner. The beginner will press either on his larynx—on *u = oo*(7), or on the base of the tongue—on *i*(1). Moreover, the *i*(1) is too great an effort for the soft palate of the beginner, especially for tenors. Though the soft palate must be trained to work, it should not be fatigued at the beginning of the training. The *u = oo*(7) tends to misplace the voice and corrupt it;[35] but, worst of all, it tires the larynx.

Therefore, one should never practice entire exercises on *i*(1) or on *u = oo*(7), and, more or less, these vowels should be avoided until the *solfeggi* and text singing are studied.[36]

When an exercise proves successful and is sung with ease on *a*(4), this exercise should be used for the other vowels: *é*(2), *è*(3), *ó*(5), *ò*(6). Thereafter mixed exercises employing *é, è, a, ó, ò* plus the shut sound[37] in all combinations and variations should be started. But all mixed exercises should be practiced solely on *a*(4) to start with, to be repeated at the end with the shut voice.

Pure, wordless agility is always executed exclusively on *a*(4). It would show very bad taste to sing the pure agility of a cadence (see p. 75) on any other vowel.

The Italian language has only these seven pure vowels. The English language

---

[35] See Appendix, §2.d) Hooting Voice (*Voce Tubata*), p. 131.
[36] See Part II, Chapter I: A: §4. The Study of *Solfeggi* and Text Singing, p. 70.
[37] See this Part, §9. The Shut Voice, p. 23.

uses very few pure vowels and many impure vowels and diphthongs. These impure vowels and diphthongs are the result of speaking with the throat more or less tightened and closed. With an open throat one cannot produce them. The Italian language has none.

Italian is the language of the open throat and therefore the most *cantabile* of all languages. Because of this, the Italians are the most singing people on earth.

Of course, no nation can be expected to sing in Italian only. While singing in English the student may be advised to divide the diphthongs into their respective vowels. I do **not** advise anybody to do this. The English language is too rich in diphthongs of all varieties, too rich in impure vowels, and too scanty in pure vowels to succeed with such system. Besides, I believe that every tongue should be sung naturally, clearly and with all finesse of a cultured enunciation.

When the voice of an English-speaking singer is resting well above the breath in a sure and firm manner and his throat is open and free as the throat of an Italian educated in a good school, when he does not find any difficulty with Bel Canto (to which I have dedicated almost the entire second part of this manual), then he should become accustomed to singing in English, his native tongue.

§11

The Consonants and Their Study

The consonants are produced by organs which have a very great influence on phonation (tone production), **although they do not create tone** (musical sound).

Therefore, one should not start any text singing before the voice (male or female) is faultlessly placed above the breath[38] and maturing into brilliance, body, and flexibility. Moreover, the "entire" vocal apparatus must already be both strong and supple, if one is to have no difficulty whatever with enunciation throughout the entire range—this means, of course, if one wishes not merely to sing, but to sing well.

The consonants were divided by the great masters of the old Italian school into the true and the so-called semiconsonants.

I.   CONSONANTS (TRUE CONSONANTS)

The true consonants may be subdivided, according to the organs that produce them, into six groups:

---

[38] With diligent and intelligent **daily** training, three to six months are needed to place the voice above the breath and only two to three years until **such** a student is ready for the study of his opera repertoire.

1) Labials. . . . . Ital. b (*bello*); p (*polvere*).
       Eng. b (but); p (peach).
2) Labial—dentals. . . . . .Ital. v (*vino*); f (*fiore*).
       Eng. v (visit); f (fine).
3) Dental—linguals. . . . . Ital. d (*del*); t (*tuo*); z (*zio*).
       Eng. d (dear); t (to); z (zest); th (the).
4) Dental—lingual—palatals. . . . . Ital. s soft (*riso*); s hard (*sogno*).
       Eng. s soft (has); s hard (sin).
5) Lingual—palatals. . . . . Ital. sce (*scelto*) sci (*scienza*); c soft (*ciò*); g soft (*gente*).
       Eng. sh (she); ch (chance); g soft (general); j (juice).
6) Lingual—gutturals. . . . . Ital. c hard (*capo*); q (*questo*); g hard (*gola*).
       Eng. c hard = k (cool, kind); q (quick); g hard (give).

Also, they may be subdivided according to the resulting sound into two groups:

1) Explosives or Stops: b, p; d, t; hard c = k; q (qu); hard g; f.
2) Sibilants or Hisses:
   a) soft s; hard s; Ital. sc $\begin{cases} \text{e } (scelto) \\ \text{i } (scienza) \end{cases}$ = Fr. ch (*chez*) = Eng. sh (she) = Ger. sch (*schon*); x; z; Ital. soft c (*ciò*) = Eng. ch (chance); etc.; in short all "s" sounds in their manifold variations and modifications.
   b) soft g; j (different in Eng. [*juice*], Fr. [*je*], Ger. [*ja*], etc., and not used in Ital.); Eng. th; Ital., Fr., Eng. v (*vino, vin,* visit) = Ger. w (*Wein*). (The Eng. w, originating in the eleventh century from "double u," usually is considered not to be a consonant but is classed as a semi*vowel;* regardless of any pigeonholing, it is a velarized, unsingable sound.)

Every singer who strives for artistry has to have complete control over his vocal apparatus. For this reason he should become familiar with both classifications of the consonants. But neither of these classifications nor a thorough analysis of each consonant, which may easily be found in a first-class dictionary, will help in the text singing of any language.

The very first fact students, teachers and coaches have to realize concerning the true consonants is that they are not singable. **It is absolutely impossible to sing true consonants.** Although it is indispensable to formalize them precisely, one must not linger on them; otherwise, the singing loses its legato at every stop, and the emission of vocal "music" is replaced by a hiss at every sibilant.

To attain a perfect (clear and natural) enunciation of all consonants, regardless of the text's language, and one that will never interfere with the flow of real "singing," and, consequently, will be easy on the voice producer, I follow the tracks of the wise masters of bygone days. When the student has learned to vocalize correctly with an open throat and *dans le masque,* I guide him with the utmost patience until he catches the **mental sensation** of pronouncing, in a precise and brief manner, each consonant above the breath within the focus of the resonances (*dans le masque*). I teach him to do so both in singing and speaking. By means of such a method that may seem just as absurd and is just as helpful as that of the sound attack[39] he will not lose the support of the voice during the formation of the consonants. The action of the larynx is not interrupted with each syllable, and, above all, the tension and the contraction of the vocal cords do not lose their continuity and regularity.

By always **mentally** enunciating the consonants within the focus of the resonances, the well-known and most important MORSO DEL SUONO [bite into the sound] will develop automatically though slowly.

The reader may ask: What is this "bite into the sound" (*morso del suono*)?

The famous *morso* is nothing but the uninterrupted perfect coordination of the soft palate[40] and the larynx which is indispensable to artistic singing, and rather difficult for a beginner to maintain during the formation of consonants. Through it the whole vocal execution will be dominated and, therefore, will remain complete and clear without the voice ever losing its personal charm. Every student will grasp it slowly but surely by "mentally" producing all consonants above the breath in the focus of the resonances, **if his lower jaw has been trained to be extremely mobile in its sockets.**

The study of the consonants should coincide with the study of solmization, to be perfected by the study of Vaccai.[41]

Then an Italian song of the old school should be chosen, one by Scarlatti or Pergolesi, for example.[42]

The study of an *old Italian opera* should begin only after the student has learned to syllabify well and, also on his high notes, without difficulty. I say "old" for reasons which will be understood after reading the second part of this manual, and "Italian" because this language is rich in vowels, sparing in true consonants, and contains no words that end on a true consonant.

---

[39] See this Part, §5. Sound Attack, p. 12.

[40] See this Part, §9. The Shut Voice, p. 23.

[41] See Part II, Chapter I: A: §4. The Study of *Solfeggi* and Text Singing, p. 70; the reader will find there not merely the study of the *solfeggi* but also how text singing was taught by a great master of the past.

[42] Alessandro Scarlatti, *il grande trapanese* (1649–1725), disciple of Gian Giacomo Carissimi (1604?–1674), was born in Trapani, Sicily, in 1649, and not—as most English biographies state—in Palermo, Sicily, in 1658, or 1659, or 1660. He was a famous singer, harpist, and cembalist. He is still with us as a composer. Also, he was an outstanding teacher, who counted among his master pupils Leonardo Leo, Francesco Durante, and his son Domenico Scarlatti. Of his many operas, *Eraclea* (1700) and *Griselda* (1721) were the best. He wrote more than two hundred Masses, many still in use. His simple, melodious songs are exquisite. Every cultured coach should be familiar with: *Sento nel core—certo dolore; Già il sole dal Gange; Se Florindo è fedele; Son tutta duolo.* Last, but not least, may I mention the gorgeous little song *O cessate di piagarmi.*

Giovanni Battista Pergolesi (1710–1736), who died of phthisis when he was twenty-

Returning to the study of the true consonants, I would like to add at this point that a double consonant is always pronounced on the second syllable.

O mio ba-bbi- no   O mio bab-bi- no
right pronunciation   wrong pronunciation

So much for the Italian pronunciation of the true consonants.

In English the student must, as often as possible, produce the end consonant of the first syllable on the beginning of the second, etc., naturally **without falling into the habit of dragging.**[43] He will use the *cesura* which I shall explain while speaking of the English "h"[44] only in words starting with an "h" or when the nature and/or the accumulation of consonants makes it necessary for clear pronunciation.

In your eyes   a   bright dis-dain.   written

I-nyou-reye-sa   bright di-sdain.   executed

cesura   *a flauto* but clearly

It can be seen from these two examples that Italian is easier on the vocal organ in singing. It is the language of song. Therefore, I advise all English-speaking students to study singing in Italian in order that, when their bite into the sound is perfected, they will be able to sing well in English.

---

six, was at thirteen an outstanding violinist. Among his many teachers were two famous disciples of the just mentioned Alessandro Scarlatti: Leonardo Leo (1694–1745) and Francesco Durante (1684–1755). Like Alessandro Scarlatti he too is still in our midst. We love his *Serva Padrona* in which the typical signs of the opera of those days—irony, spirit, vivacity, and caricature—make us forget our burdens and sorrows. His *Stabat Mater,* written for soprano, contralto, choir, violins, and organ, which contains no less than six solos, four duets, and two fugues, has survived two centuries of enormous artistic evolution—and this because of its beauty and richness of fantasy. His songs, too, have for us the charm they had for our ancestors. Recommended as an asset in a female concert repertory is *Se tu m' ami, se tu sospiri.* The young artist will surely not regret it.

[43] See Part II, Chapter I: A: §2. The Beginning of the Study of Bel Canto and Legato Singing, p. 38.

[44] See this §, III. The H, p. 32.

II.   SEMICONSONANTS

There are four consonants (l, m, n, r) that are singable. They, therefore, are called semiconsonants.

Whoever tries to sing l, m, n, or r, then tries to sing p or b, etc. will understand what I mean.

"M" is a naso-labial semiconsonant. It is the easiest consonant in all languages, just as the *a* in father is the most natural vowel for all people. Therefore, the first word that all babies of every race on earth say is "ma-ma."

Some people with very heavy lips make this semiconsonant explosive. The student's attention should be drawn to his defect only when he starts to sol-fa.[45] But then he should be corrected every single time he fails and forces the "m," which will be most apparent when a *solfeggio* starts with *mi*. This forceful attack on the "m" that misplaces the voice must be overcome before any study of repertoire can be started with success.

"N" is a naso-dental semiconsonant. It is not so easy as "m"; it may be of help for heavy voices, especially as in "ny," like in onion, canyon.

But due to its abuse in studying, the student easily acquires the nasal habit; therefore, one should be careful.

"L" and "R" are twins; they are lingual semiconsonants.

"L" is produced by the tip of the tongue and does not require any explanation. It is so easy that generally it is the first consonant to be used in the study of singing. Only persons with a defective frenum have a faulty "l".

"R" is produced differently in different tongues.

The Italian "R": the muscles of the tongue and the anterior muscles of the larynx are so strong and elastic that they make the **tip of the tongue** vibrate against the hard palate as a drumstick vibrates on the drumhead. With such an "r" sound, emission is not disturbed, and *glissandi* as well as clean-cut scales can and should be accomplished. For all English-speaking students this will be a most helpful exercise if employed daily but in moderation, and should be started long before the study of the consonants.

The French "R": This is produced like the Italian "r", but the muscles of the tongue are so weak that the tip of the tongue vibrates much less.

The German "R": This is formed at the **base of the tongue** and gives the voice a harsh and guttural color.

The English "R": This is formed at the base of the tongue, as is the German "r", but it is often so neglected that it is hardly heard.

III.   THE *H*

The Italians and French do not pronounce the "H". For the Germanic tongues it is a little toneless expulsion of air produced by a shock of the glottis.

---

[45] See Part II, Chapter I: A: §4. The Study of *Solfeggi* and Text Singing, p. 70

From what has been explained up to this point, it becomes obvious that a Germanic "h" cannot be admitted in singing, because in singing no air must ever be expelled, and not even the slightest breath of air released which does not serve to make the vocal cords vibrate, thus producing tone. Therefore, the toneless (tone = musical sound) Germanic "h" not only is not singable, but, being an expulsion of air and produced by a shock of the glottis, it is antagonistic to the very function of singing.[46]

We have the same verb in Italian: *avere*
French: *avoir*
English: have ⎫ "h" produced by a shock
German: *haben* ⎭ of the glottis

Hence those who wish to sing in English or in any other Germanic tongue, with an Italian voice emission, must reckon with the problem of the "h". The "h" must not be enunciated by means of a shock of the glottis as in the Germanic manner, and it cannot be done in any Italian manner, being foreign to the Italian tongue. Unfortunately, without it one cannot sing in English.

Then what is to be done?

One should use, before the vowel that follows an "h", a very brief but clear *cesura* in singing, and attack the vowel that follows the "h" with extreme smoothness and precision. By the *cesura* we understand a tiny interruption of sound, while sustaining and retaining the air of one and the same breath. For those who do not comprehend, it is a tiny interruption of sound during which **no air whatsoever** must be emitted from the lungs. Those who know French need only use the *h aspiré* as in *la honte*. It is the same thing.

written

My   heart   is

executed

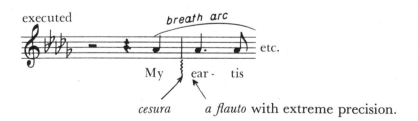

cesura   *a flauto* with extreme precision.

---

[46] All the Latin languages weigh the syllables and that is why these tongues are so melodious. All the Germanic languages accent the syllables by means of shocks of the glottis, and that is why these languages are more or less guttural or harsh.

§12

The Importance of Vocal Technique

So far I have not spoken of singing itself but have limited myself, after a very short and simple explanation of the vocal organs, to explaining exactly and minutely what to do in order to use the vocal organs according to the ideas of the old Italian school.

A perfect vocal technique (voice emission) is the basis for any artistic singing technique, even if the singing technique is a different one from the famous technique of Bel Canto to which I dedicate the first chapter of the second part of this manual.

It must be understood that in the actual teaching of singing, a division between vocal technique and singing technique cannot be made. Vocal technique will be learned while singing, and singing technique can be attained while mastering the faultless old Italian vocal technique.

I have made this inartistic division for the sake of a fruitful explanation of a subject so antagonistic to rigid analysis as is the abstract art of singing.

Part II

THE EDUCATION OF THE ARTIST

The artist is a being whose soul dwells beyond the gates of reality, yet one who is able to mold his visions into vivid reality. *Art never facilitates its creator's life;* on the contrary —like most profound love—it is a precious burden, cherished by its bearer above all else.

CHAPTER I

The Study of Bel Canto

A: THE TECHNIQUE OF BEL CANTO

§1

Explanation of the Expression "Bel Canto"

Many people believe that "Bel Canto" is the famous Italian singing method of bygone days. Instead, and although Bel Canto means literally *beautiful singing,* it is by no means the terminology for any method of voice production, but refers to the superb polyphonic and melismatic (florid, embellished, ornamented) style of music that emerged from the medieval crude polyphonic music—the discant.[1] After many unsatisfactory attempts to overcome the latter's problems of counterpoint, this new style appeared for the first time clearly in Venice and with young Giovanni Gabrieli of the Venetian school (1557–1612, entombed in S. Stefano, Venice). At the turn of the sixteenth century the grace of its spirit had already influenced Florence and the Apostolic Chapel,[2] the new center of the Roman polyphonic school. By the end of the seventeenth century Bel Canto had developed into Europe's dominant style. Although its flexibility was at times abused in this epoch of vocal glorification by some autocratic and vainglorious interpreters, Bel Canto always was treated with creative skill by its composers, the greatest in musical history, until about the middle of the nineteenth century. Its last exponent was Rossini (1794–1868) whose compositions are to be considered the supreme incarnation of Bel Canto of the nineteenth

---

[1] A few lines about the discant are to be found in this Chapter: A: §2.V.a) Trills, Introduction, p. 56.

[2] Often the unilateral conception is encountered that the word "chapel" means only a sanctuary of worship, but, besides having other meanings, the word "chapel" also refers to the entire staff of musicians—choir singers, soloists, composers, instrumentalists and so forth—attached to the court of an ecclesiastic or secular sovereign or even a nobleman. Apostolic Chapel signifies much more, because the latter expression embraces the entire staff of dignitaries, including the College of Cardinals, the patriarchs, all assistants of the pontifical throne, in short, all who rank as members of the pope's household, and naturally including the musicians.

century. This splendor of the Rossinian Bel Canto started to disappear rapidly about 1830. Already Bellini (1801–1835) and Donizetti (1797–1848) no longer wrote in pure Bel Canto. Both had an expressive largo style, that of Donizetti being more vibrant and romantic. Finally, with Verdi (1813–1901), who began with the Donizetti style, the last shades of Bel Canto vanished forever.

The Bel Canto style brought to perfection the pure beauty of tone, the clarity and agility of the voice.

It encouraged the artist to invent ornaments with an infinite number of variations for one and the very same melody.

In order to arrive at the elasticity of throat and mind that was indispensable for meeting the demands of this epoch—the greatest in Italian singing—the teachers of singing who oftentimes were not only vocal virtuosos but excellent composers too, wrote special exercises, called *solfeggi*,[3] intended suitably to train the future artist.

Since neither before nor after this period the artist's throat had to be so free and elastic, nor so well trained, it can be understood that in order to loosen and train a throat which today must sing more or less modern music, there is nothing better than the study of this musical style of the past and its most perfect technique.

§2
The Beginning of the Study of Bel Canto and Legato Singing

To be able to execute correctly Bel Canto's masterpieces, first of all its famous technique has to be studied seriously and to perfection. The study of this technique starts with the study of legato singing from the very first exercise which the beginner sings in the limited compass of his voice, with the vowel *a* (father, art).[4] Therefore, the study of Bel Canto may be said to begin with the first correct singing lesson.[5]

What does legato singing mean?

To sing legato means to pass from one note to another cleanly, readily, and naturally. There should be neither the slightest voice irregularity nor voice interruption (sound vacuum) between two notes; also the voice should not be dragged

---

[3] See this Chapter: A: §4. The Study of *Solfeggi* and Text Singing, p. 70.

[4] See Part I, §6. II, The Timbre of the Voice, p. 20 and Part I, §10, The Study of the Vowels and Diphthongs and Their Application to English Singing, p. 25.

[5] Simultaneously, the old teachers commenced training their new pupils in a system of artistic gymnastics, which helped not only to make the young body elastic and resistant to the strain of the future profession, but gave the student a perfect sense of balance, leading him to that mastery of his own movements, which is indispensable for an easy artistic poise; our teachers should not be less provident. For the study of other side subjects see this Part, Chapter II: §1. The Study of Music and Languages, p. 85.

from one note to another. No matter how long or short the interval—no clicking should ever be heard! In Italy it is said: "Who does not sing legato does not sing," because he who does not know how to tie or connect smoothly one note to another without dragging the sounds does not know how to control his breath. Therefore, he either shouts, wails, or cackles, but does "not sing."

The study of the legato is not a special study, since one cannot place the voice above the breath without seeing to it that all notes of one and the same phrase are faultlessly connected or tied to one another.[6] Consequently, every well-placed voice will be legato.

Here is a graphic design to help in understanding the legato:

good   bad   bad

legato   dragged (*strisciato*)   not legato—not connected,
and its abuse ruins the voice.

* notes in mind

In order to succeed in having a free and elastic throat, ready for all types of singing, in the beginning the pupil must not tire himself with long notes, but must work only on the legato agility (fluency).

There is no fixed rule for exercises. It all depends on the disposition of the pupil as to the best time to do this or that.

But it is necessary for all students immediately to begin the study of the *scalette*,[7] then—as soon as possible—to start with the study of the semitones,[8] and of all the other intervals.[9]

The study of legato singing is terminated with the study of the sustained notes,[10] and of the *portamenti*.[11]

I.   THE SCALETTE

The ascending agility is more difficult than the descending one. The voice of the beginner on ascending slows up, on descending it hurries.

Do not lose the rhythm!

---

[6] See Part I, §6.I. The Registers and Their Union, p. 14.

[7] Of course, first on the descending scale only.

[8] See this §, II. The Semitones and the Chromatic Scales, p. 41.

[9] See this §, III. The Study of the Intervals, p. 44.

[10] See this §, VI. Sustained Notes, p. 63.

[11] See this §, VII. The *Portamenti*, p. 66.

When a descending scale sounds out of tune, one may be sure that the descending semitones are going flat.

* Attention!

Do not make any trailing sounds! Retain the breath![12]

As many combinations can be made of *scalette* [partial scales] as there are lessons. It is impossible to enumerate them all. The more flexible the throat becomes, the more often must they change, in order that both **the throat and the mind** acquire the maximum of elasticity and readiness, two musts for becoming an artist and not merely a singer.

All exercises are to be executed on the whole compass of the student's voice, and with extreme care of the rhythm.

Here is a simple fifth used as a basic exercise on *scalette* with five of its many developments, just to give an idea of how one should study.

Basic exercise.

Development, sample 1.

Development, sample 2.

---

[12] See Part I, §7. Sound Detachment, p. 21.

Development, sample 3.

Sample 3 for Negro Voices. (The entire exercise on one breath.)

Development, sample 4.

Development, sample 5.

II. THE SEMITONES AND THE CHROMATIC SCALES

The semitones are difficult for the student, and many beginners feel this. Seldom is the modern voice teacher able to help. Therefore, the following pages deal with this important subject in detail.

The smallest musical interval that the human ear is able to perceive is called a comma (Gr. *komma*).

The interval of a whole tone $\begin{smallmatrix}(C-D)\\(do-re)\end{smallmatrix}$ is composed of nine commas (atoms of the voice).

From one semitone to another there are five commas if major, and four if minor. The ancients knew this very well; the Greeks called a five-comma interval *apotomē* [a cutting off] and a four-comma interval *leimma* [remnant] and *diesis*. The latter term still lives in its old meaning; it is the Italian term for a "sharp" (♯).

Two intervals of major semitones
(five commas)

Two intervals of minor semitones
(four commas)

Here follows a graphic explanation of the semitones, to make it very clear that a "C sharp" (*do diesis*) is not the same sound as a "D flat" or an "E sharp" the same as an "F", and so forth.

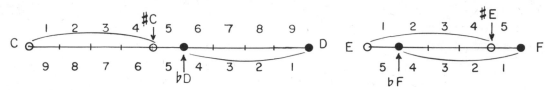

A "C sharp" is a "C" augmented by a minor semitone, and a "D flat" is a "D" diminished—softened—by a minor semitone, and so forth.[13]

Because of the slight difference between major and minor semitones

is not equal to

This slight difference between semitones, however, does not exist on the well-tempered piano, where for instance a "C sharp" (♯) has the same number of vibrations as a "D flat" (♭); and an "E sharp" (♯) the same number as an "F natural" ( ). For this reason the human voice sounds more beautiful if accompanied by stringed instruments played by bow.

A beginner should never sing chromatic passages without having first established where the minor and the major semitones are; also, he should learn to keep the last note of the chromatic passage well fixed in mind.

Besides the pure chromatic scales, I use countless exercises to help the student

---

[13] This is why one must never transpose a composition written by the composer in a sharp key to one in flats, nor, of course, transpose a flat key into a sharp one. One would change the color of the piece. The sharp key, the raised key, is brighter and the flat key, the lowered key, is softer and more sentimental.

[14] i = minor semitone; a = major semitone

acquire facility with semitones; here are six samples of them. They are to be executed on the entire range of the voice and with extreme care of the rhythm.

Accent the first of each group without kicking the sound!

See this Chapter: A: §4. The Study of *Solfeggi,* exercise 4, p. 73.

___

[15] This exercise is for a beginner and to be started as soon as possible.

[16] This exercise is by Father Martini. The Franciscan monk Giambattista Martini, of Bologna (1706–1784), educated by Bologna's best musicians and philosophers, was a composer, a renowned teacher, and a recognized savant, often consulted deferentially by outstanding composers. It was Martini who insisted over and over again that every composition first and last must sing, and that the counterpoint is written to the plain chant, not vice versa, as was done in Martini's days, seemingly just as often as today by composers whose inner ear lacks song. Among Martini's pupils are to be enumerated N. Jommelli, G. Tartini, G. B. Mancini (see this Part, footnote 26, p. 60), L. Gibelli (see Part

To many persons all semitones sound alike, because—to say it politely—their ears are not sensitive enough to hear the difference in tone color between the sharp and the flat key and the slight difference in pitch between major and minor semitones. I would like to bring to their attention Ptolemy's (see p. 71) musical law that neither the octave itself, nor any musical interval within it, is divisible into equal parts (*Harmonikōn biblia 3,* book I, chap. 13). More recently, in 1723, in his treatise *Opinioni de cantori antichi e moderni,* Tosi (see p. 121) explained nature's musical laws regarding the semitones for his contemporaries. The same has been done in a modern manner in this manual.

FOR VOICE TEACHERS: Start this most important part of vocal education not only by explaining the difference between major and minor semitones, but also by demonstrating the difference with your voice. Never play on the piano each single chromatic step of an exercise on chromatic passages; give the chord only. But better, far better, show with your voice the correct execution of the chromatic passage that you want your student to sing, and let him repeat it under your guidance. For today's average students you may need much patience, and you may have to demonstrate over and over again. The "born-musician" never needs such help; instinctively he follows the laws of nature, and his chromatic scales are faultlessly clean before he starts to study singing.

III.   THE STUDY OF THE INTERVALS

There is not much to be said on this subject, though one should be extremely careful about it. Many lovely pieces among the *solfeggi*[17] are most suitable for this study, but one should not wait to start it until the student begins the *solfeggi.*

On placing the voice all intervals should be studied. There is no fixed rule. It is for the teacher to determine when the pupil is ready to attempt the jump of the augmented second,[18] tritone (*tritonus*),[18] sixth, octave, ninth, or the tenth without displacing the voice.

Intervals should always be studied in conjunction with scales, since when studied alone they tire the voice of the student too much.

The study of the interval of the ninth and the tenth, which is important to the

---

III, footnote 38, p. 107), F. G. Bertoni (see Part III, footnote 49, p. 117). His favorite disciple was Stanislao Mattei (1730–1825), the teacher of Donizetti and of Rossini. Father Martini and Stanislao Mattei were the last great exponents of Bologna's famous music school. When fourteen year old Mozart (1756–1791) came to this "cradle for musicians" Martini recognized in him a genius. In his kindness Martini not only made young Mozart a member of Bologna's Philharmonic Academy but also wrote secretly for him the obligatory composition of admission. Father Martini has left us the first three volumes of a *History of Music.* These three volumes treat the vicissitudes of music among the nations of antiquity. It is the best history of that period we possess. The fourth volume, treating medieval music, still is in manuscript.

[17] See this Chapter: A: §4. The Study of *Solfeggi* and Text Singing, p. 72.

modern singer, does not at all belong to the real Bel Canto style. Therefore, by rights it should not be treated in this section. But since the jumps of the ninth and tenth require a very accurate and long training of the throat, and since an artist of today finds himself obliged to sing ninths and tenths, I take care to train my pupils in the execution of these jumps as early as possible. I have, therefore, thought it opportune to include this subject, although it does not belong to the study of Bel Canto.

Here are twenty-eight of the many different exercises on intervals that I have my pupils practice before the *solfeggi*. If studied at the right moment, they do not cause fatigue, and they prepare both mind and voice for the difficult task ahead. All of them are to be executed on the entire range of the voice, and in a perfect "legato."

See this Chapter: A: §2. IV. c) The Composite Leaning Notes and the Turn: B) 1., p. 53.

[18] I have noted that there are many who do not know the meaning of an augmented second and of the term tritone, *tritonus* or augmented fourth.
Here is an example of each:

augmented second.

augmented fourth, tritone, *tritonus* (the musical term L. *tonus*, Gr. *tonos* —meaning our whole tone).

Both intervals need much practice and attention by a beginner, since in order to produce them with ease, it is necessary that both the throat and mind be trained to these intervals.

See this Chapter: A: §4. The Study of *Solfeggi,* exercise 2, p. 72.

See this Chapter: A: §2.IV.b) The Crush Note, p. 51.

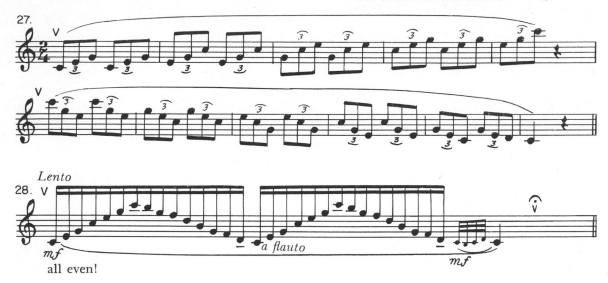

all even!

Our twentieth century music—besides this basic musical training—calls for the education of the student's ear in modern harmonies. One should never forget therefore, to include in the training exercises which will help the young artist when singing modern music. I believe that such exercises are most important, and extreme care should be given to the selection of them. Otherwise the young voice will become jaded, and lose its freshness.

I have not included here any exercises on the two whole-tone scales favored by Debussy, and on modern modulations in which I train my pupils most seriously after their registers are amalgamated and once they begin to have perfect breath control. Such exercises would be out of place in this manual.

IV.   THE MUSICAL EMBELLISHMENTS

The musical embellishments, often referred to as "graces," are vocal or instrumental ornaments not essential to the melody or harmony of a composition. They are used to embroider the music.

We can trace musical embellishments of all kinds, we can trace even quarter tone graces* as a most important factor in music as far back as the ancient Greeks of the sixth century B.C., when the use of music with the emphasis on melismatics (orna-

---

* It would be far more appropriate to call the quarter tone a three-comma tone, because it consists of three commas. It was used exclusively as a grace in the enharmonic music of the ancient Greeks; some of our composers try their skill at this interval in a rather futile manner; it is foreign to the superb purity of the Bel Canto, and, therefore, it would be out of place to treat it in this manual.

For "comma" see this Chapter: A: §2. II. The Semitones and the Chromatic Scales, p. 41.

ments) has been, since the genius Pythagoras of Samos, well known to the sage physicians of ancient Greece for calming bodily pains and for soothing all tensions of the nervous system.

a) **THE SIMPLE LEANING NOTE (*Appoggiatura Semplice*)** is the simplest ornament in music. As the word "leaning" suggests, it is a note upon which the voice (human as well as instrumental) leans or rests. It may be outside the harmony but must resolve into a real harmonic note. It is no other than the musical accent that falls constantly on the beat of the measure, thus enhancing both melody and rhythmical flow.

The leaning note may be inferior or superior. If it is inferior, it is a minor second (a major semitone); if it is superior, it is either a minor second or a major second (a whole tone). Also, whether ascending or descending, the leaning note may be, if necessary, any note of the chord itself, regardless of the interval.

The leaning note steals its very value from the real note that follows it. It is sung or played just as a real note, but it is usually written in a smaller type.[19]

written

executed

Its duration varies. If the measure is even, the leaning note absorbs half of the value of the principal note.

written

executed

If the principal note is followed by a dot, the leaning note robs two-thirds of the value of the principal note.

written

executed **and never otherwise!**

In the recitative[20] the *appoggiatura* absorbs the entire value of the syllable upon which it falls, thus losing its embellishing character. It is neither written nor marked,

---

[19] In modern music, as in some modern editions of old music (Mozart), we find it written as a real note.

written

[20] See this Chapter: B: §1. The Recitative, p. 80.

but it would be a complete violation of style not to use it. Without *appoggiatura* the recitative would become very monotonous. It is the leaning note that gives it life and grace.

The *appoggiatura* must always be executed in legato only.

Where the *appoggiatura* cannot ascend, it cannot descend and *vice versa.*[21]

b) **THE CRUSH NOTE (*Acciaccatura*)** is a very short note that precedes a real note—*no sooner produced than released.*

It is written as a small cut note  .

The average American music student calls this grace a "short leaning note"; but such a translation of *acciaccatura* (*acciaccare* means to crush) is inappropriate, because the voice—human as well as instrumental—**never leans,** never rests on this embellishment. It is exactly the opposite; the voice scarcely touches this grace.

The crush note may be inferior or superior and may be any note of the scale (see exercise 21, p. 48), but for the most part this grace is superior and either a major second (a whole tone) or a minor second (a major semitone). The artist of today should use it only if he finds it written, and should sing it exactly as asked for.

For a short period, the music for keyboard instruments also knew a crush note a semitone below the principal note that was struck, not before, but at exactly the same instant as the principal note; this grace had to be immediately released, so that only the principal note sustained the sound. Because of this simultaneous attack of the grace and the principal note, the Germans called this form of *acciaccatura, Zusammenschlag* (*zusammenschlagen* means to strike together). For some time it was much in vogue with German organists, but it was rejected in France and derided in Italy.

Italy's *acciaccatura,* the charming grace that still fills our modern music, always precedes the principal note. It has to be executed in legato only, and with dancing liveliness—*con brio*, because it should bring sparkling brightness into the music.

If the note that carries a superior crush note is brief itself, and, in addition, is tied to another descending note, the voice should take both the grace and the real note with a stimulating impetus, thereafter resting smoothly on the third note and prolonging the latter. Such embellishment is to be used exclusively on descending.

written   executed

---

[21] One of the many rules established by the contraltist (eunuch contralto) Pier Francesco Tosi in his famous treatise *Opinioni de' cantori antichi e moderni,* Bologna, 1723. For his elaborated biography see Part III, The *Musici,* Tosi, p. 121. For an exact understanding of the expression "contraltist" read Part III, Survey, p. 91.

c) **The Composite Leaning Notes (*Appoggiature Composte*) and the Turn (*Gruppetto*):** I have spoken of the simple leaning notes which are so easy that they require no special study. Even the composite leaning notes (*appoggiature composte*) do not offer difficulty to the throat.

The composite leaning notes most in use are the *gruppetti* or turns. Two centuries ago such a *gruppetto* was called *caudatus*.

The *gruppetto* [turn] is an embellishment composed of any two or three consecutive leaning notes, descending or ascending.

half-turn: whole turn:
(*mezzo-gruppetto:*)   (*gruppetto:*)

The signs for the whole turn are ∽ (⋎ superior *caudatus*) or ∽ (⋏ inferior *caudatus*). (*Caudatus* means caudated, tailed.)

∽ and ∽ indicate different executions of the turn.

The sign of the turn can occupy three different places: in front (A), above (B), or at the end (C) of the note to which it belongs.

A) 1. ∽ in front of a note: written  means   ;

executions:

I say rarely because the value of the turn should seldom go below ♪ = 100.

If the note that carries the turn is very short, turn and principal note will best take the same value.

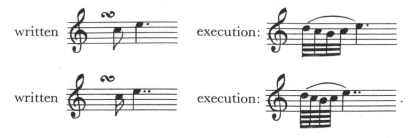

B) 2. above a note: written means ;

executions: etc.

written   executions: etc.

written   best execution:

written   executions:

etc.

rarely

C) 1. at the end of a note: Every turn has to end on the note which it embel-lishes.   written

executions:

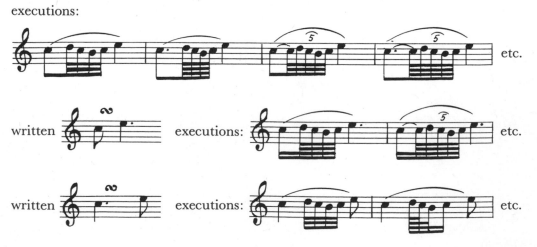

etc.

written   executions: etc.

written   executions: etc.

C)   2. ∽ at the end of a note: written

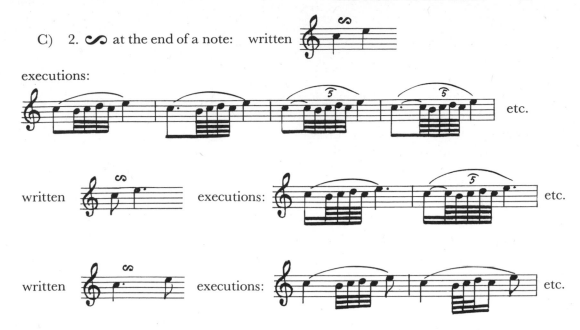

It is evident that the execution of the turn leaves the artist freedom concerning rhythm and speed. He should choose according to the character of the musical phrase, and not according to his personal temperament.

No artist is permitted to change the succession of the embellishing notes prescribed by the composer as many seem to believe.

The artist is free to choose either of the two forms (∾ or ∽) in the few cases where the old style (executed to suit our modern taste) allows to embellish a note by a turn which is not marked.

Also, he is entirely free to decide whether the high note of the turn, sung as a major second or as a minor second, will give the beat more grace and lightness. But he will have to watch not to distort the tonality of the musical phrase through his decision! Concerning the low note, one has no choice whatsoever. **The low note of a turn has to be a minor second.** Whenever a minor second in the downward movement of a turn offends the ear, the execution of a turn is out of place, because between the low note and the middle note there must always be the distance of a minor second, and **the whole turn can never go beyond the limit of a minor third.** All musicians—not only singers—should very carefully obey this rule and never fail to apply it, because in stepping beyond the limit of a minor third the turn loses all the enchanting grace and lightness so characteristic of Bel Canto.

These are fundamental Bel Canto rules which every artist has to follow carefully if he desires to execute the compositions written in this famous style in the correct manner.

In the past, the composite leaning notes permitted a great many variations. The student need not concern himself with them, as they offer no difficulty whatever to a voice placed above the breath. On the contrary, they rest such a voice.

Here follow a few examples.

These composite leaning notes were used *a piacere* [at discretion] continuously. They sometimes even took the place of the simple leaning note in the recitative.[22] Today taking such liberty would be very bad taste and would make the singer ridiculous, but one may use them *a piacere* when creating one's own cadences (*cadenze,* cadenzas), of which I will speak later on—in this Chapter: A: §5, p. 75.

Half-turn, turn, and composite leaning notes of all combinations always steal their value from the note to which they belong. They should be executed—although generally in utmost rapidity—with careful precision and grace, and without ever breaking the melodic line or the rhythm of the phrase. This permits their being slowed down on the finale of a phrase or piece.

V. TRILLS, *VOLATE, MORDENTI*

a) **TRILLS:** The trill, the most charming adornment in singing, was well known to the ancient Greek and Roman singers. The Greeks called it *strobīlos,* and it filled all ancient melismatic singing, which I treated at the beginning of the previous chapter (IV. The Musical Embellishments). The Romans called it *sonus vibrans,* and it was just as cherished in ancient Rome as soon as Rome started to imbibe the culture of Greece. It was also used throughout medieval Europe, up to the beginning of the fourteenth century, under the name of *pressus.* But with the medieval new and primitive polyphonic music—the discant—that emerged in the thirteenth century as the Gregorian chant vanished, vocal ability declined more and more, and the *pressus* was neglected. It disappeared entirely in the fourteenth century, because the crude discant with its extremely hard harmonies had become the dominating musical style, and especially because Pope John XXII (1316–1334) in Avignon strictly forbade in a Brief "all melismatics of any kind." The trill was reintroduced with its actual name into Europe's music only in 1592 by the contraltist (eunuch contralto) Gian Luca Conforti who is treated in Part III of this manual, after the latter's admission to the Pontifical Chapel, which, finally having matured into noble simplicity and beauty, claimed again vocal perfection of its singers. Since then the trill has remained an essential musical ornament.

Tosi[23] said concerning the trill: "He who lacks it or cannot perform it correctly, will never be a great singer." And how right he was! There are few singers today who can execute the true, birdlike trill.

The trill represents the extreme limit of celerity in vocalization. It is not composed

---

[22] See this Chapter: B: §1, The Recitative, p. 81.

[23] He is the same Pier Francesco Tosi who is mentioned in the preceding footnote 21. One should not neglect to read about his contributions to vocal art in Part III, The *Musici,* Tosi, p. 122.

of two true, real notes, as many believe, but **it is the equal vibration between one note, the real or principal note, and another, the helping or auxiliary note,** which is always higher than the real or principal note.

There are today many extremely different theories concerning the production of the auxiliary note, but there is not and never has been any doubt by serious scientists that for both auxiliary note and real note the true vocal cords do not change shape—either in length, thickness, or tension—but that they always assume the shape necessary for the production of the real note. Yet no singer ever bothered about all this. Besides, no one before the invention of the laryngoscope by Emanuele Garcia, junior,[24] knew what shape the vocal cords assumed during any vocal production. Nevertheless, the *musici*—the castrated enchanters of prelaryngoscopic days, to whom the entire Part III of this treatise is dedicated—knew how to trill as thereafter mankind was never able to do.

I know the question in many minds: But how does one trill? How is the vibration between the principal and the auxiliary note carried out?

It is done by moving the larynx regularly up and down, and the more regular and the freer these throbbing movements are, the more birdlike will sound the trill. These throbbing movements can be learned through imitation only and never through explanation. Two factors are most essential: **the teacher must have a perfect trill; the student must have a free throat.**

The student should first establish the principal note and then attack the trill itself with the auxiliary note. He must never attack with the principal note. He must always stop the throbbing of the trill on the principal note and never on the auxiliary note.

While the trill is easier for small, light voices, all trained voices must have a trill.

Sometimes a young voice, untrained and unspoiled, acquires the trill quickly; sometimes a voice, badly placed by the teacher, or inflexible by nature, has great difficulty in mastering this movement of the larynx. At all events, all voices can be trained, and every professional singer should be trained, to produce trills.

The trill will develop after the muscles of throat and neck have become strong and *very elastic* through singing above the breath, in the focus of the resonances. Whoever is master of his lower jaw, which has to be extremely mobile in its sockets, can possess a perfect trill.

Here are a few preparatory exercises for voices which have great difficulty with trills. However, such exercises should not be started before the voice is faultlessly placed above the breath, as any premature study of non-legato agility could easily handicap the student in his vocal development. I have them executed mostly on those notes of my pupil's range where I hear that the trill will develop first.

See this Chapter: A: §3.II. The *Picchettato* Agility, p. 69.

---

[24] See Part I, footnote 8, second para., p. 10.

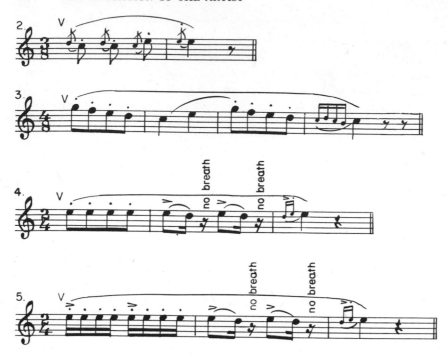

The interval between the principal note and the auxiliary note can be a major semitone, a whole tone, or any other larger interval up to a major third.

To be able to trill a major third *à la* Bernacchi or Farinelli[25] is a sign of enormous flexibility and control of the entire vocal apparatus. All sopranos should be trained to achieve this virtuosity, which in our era, of course, must never be used when singing in public. It would be a display of very bad taste and nothing else.

---

[25] Carlo Broschi, a sopranist (eunuch soprano) called Farinelli (born in Naples, 1705, died in Bologna, 1782), is generally admired as the world's supreme vocalist. He was for years the pupil of famous Porpora and strongly influenced by this most cultured musician. In 1727, when already a cherished artist, he studied under the celebrated Bernacchi of Bologna. So ravishing was his art that for nearly twenty-five years he was the prime favorite at the court of Philip V and then of Ferdinand VI of Spain. It was said that the Spanish politics of those years hung on his every whim. For his elaborated biography see Part III, The *Musici*, Farinelli, p. 104.

Nicola Antonio Porpora, the "Patriarch of Harmony" (born in Naples, 1686, died 1768—not 1766), was an extremely cultured tenor and composer who knew Latin, German, English, and French. He sang and taught in nearly all European centers of art. In Dresden (1728) Porpora taught the German crown princess Marie Antoinette. He was not Joseph Haydn's (1732–1809) voice teacher, as is emphasized in many biographies. He met Haydn in Vienna in 1752, while the latter was an unsuccessful music teacher with a broken voice. Porpora taught Haydn composition; he helped him both morally and financially, but he "never" was Haydn's voice teacher, or Haydn surely would not have ruined forever the voice of his boyhood. Among Porpora's endless chain of star

The sign for the trill is a "tr" above the note:

In the days of Farinelli,[25] eight trills were to be distinguished. Today, even when singing old music, only four of these eight forms are in use. I will, therefore, limit myself to the explanation of these four forms as used and taught by Bernacchi,[25] the "king of singers," and which since his time have passed from generation to generation.

1) THE MAJOR TRILL is a trill between two notes having an interval of a whole tone (a major second). The lower is the real or principal note, the upper the helping or auxiliary note. The throbbing starts on the auxiliary note and ends on the principal note.

From this trill arise all the others.

2) THE MINOR TRILL is a trill between two notes having an interval of a major semitone (a minor second). It cannot, of course, be a minor semitone (an augmented prime)! The lower is the principal note, the upper the auxiliary note, exactly as in the case of the major trill, and it must be executed in exactly the same manner, starting on the auxiliary note and ending on the principal note.

3) THE HALF TRILL is one of the first two trills, executed more rapidly. It must be detached soon after it is heard.

It is especially used in lively arias.

Example: *La Serva Padrona* (G. B. Pergolesi) Serpina. Aria: *Stizzoso, . . .*

Measure No. 104

-ti   e   mol -   ti   di.   Original.

___

pupils are numbered the *primadonna* Gabrielli and the sopranists: Porporino, most famous Caffarelli, and—"One God; one Farinelli." Porpora died in extreme poverty, the fate of many kind and great men. For the elaborated biographies of Porporino and Caffarelli see Part III, The *Musici,* Porporino, p. 119; Caffarelli, p. 104; for Gabrielli see Part III, footnote 51, p. 118.

Antonio Maria Bernacchi, the "king of singers" (born in Bologna, 1685, died 1756), was the favorite pupil of Francesco Antonio Pistocchi, "the founder of the Bolognese school." Bernacchi was a very celebrated sopranist (eunuch soprano) of his period, a composer, and one of the wisest teachers of all time. Some of his compositions may be found in the library of the Liceo Musicale of Bologna. Among his very many pupils of international fame are to be numbered the *primadonna* Tesi, the tenor Raaff, the *musico* Amadori, the voice teacher Mancini (see the following footnote 26), and—Farinelli "of the divine trill." For Bernacchi's elaborated biography see Part III, The *Musici,* Bernacchi, p. 103, and for the biography of his teacher Pistocchi see Part III, The *Musici,* Pistocchi, p. 118.

For an exact understanding of the expressions "sopranist" and *"musico"* read Part III, Survey, p. 91.

-ti   e   mol -   ti   di.

Variation of music
permitted by style.

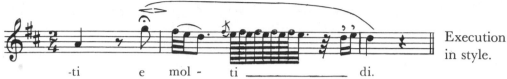

-ti   e   mol -   ti _____ di.

Execution
in style.

4) THE DOUBLE TRILL is executed by breaking up the trill without taking breath and inserting a few embellishing notes between its sections, which suffices to make two or more trills of this one trill, be it major or minor. It must be sung in a very smooth (*dolcissimo*) manner and should be used rarely. It best suits a soprano's notes

above 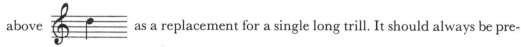 as a replacement for a single long trill. It should always be pre-

ceded by a long *messa di voce* (see p. 64) on the real note; it should never be cut off abruptly, but must be finished according to style.

Examples of Mancini[26] on the execution of the double trill:

or

_____

[26] Giambattista Mancini (1716–1800) was born in Ascoli Piceno, the Marches, and died in Vienna, Austria. There he was for nearly twenty years, from 1760 on, a teacher of singing at the imperial court of the Habsburgs—teaching princesses by the dozen. Almost nothing is known about his boyhood and youth. He studied singing from 1730 to 1732 in Naples under Leonardo Leo (1694–1745), a disciple of Alessandro Scarlatti; later, in Bologna, he studied singing with the famous Bernacchi and composition with Father Martini. Nevertheless his singing has never been mentioned, and even the category of his voice has been nowhere reported. But on the basis of the little knowledge available about him and his appearance, it is probable that he was an unsuccessful, poor *musico*. Mancini is the author of the excellent treatise on singing *Riflessioni pratiche sul canto figurato*, Milan, 1777, from which the above examples are taken. For Alessandro Scarlatti

Example of how Farinelli "of the divine trill"[25] used the double trill to end one of his famous and difficult cadences.

All four forms of trills I have just explained have to be studied on all vowels—except *i* (1) and *u = oo* (7) (see Part I, §10. p. 25)—plus the shut voice, on the whole compass of the student's voice.

The trill does not always require a preparation. This depends on the tempo, on the style of the musical phrase, and on the personal taste of the artist.

But the trill should never be ended abruptly. It always requires an ornament at its very end, which is called CLOSURE.

This closure may be a half-turn, a turn, a truncated turn, or any other kind of embellishment. In the time of the castrated singers it was even sometimes a *volata* [flight].

The choice of form for a closure of a trill depends on its location. A trill in the middle of a piece will end otherwise than the trill of a cadence (see p. 75). It also depends on its duration, according to whether it is long or short. It further depends a great deal on the musical sense of the composition; that is, if the music is sad or lively.

b) **VOLATE [Flights]:** A short, distinct, rapid and ascending scale of trills is a *volata* [flight, *roulade,* also—but less suitably—run].

The scale of a *volata* may be a diatonic or a chromatic one; of course only the previously explained major trill has to be used for trilling the latter, otherwise the *volata* will sound most offensively out of tune.

Every *volata* should be practiced first in the shut voice, and no *volata* that is not matured into a perfect jewel should be presented to the public, else the singer would risk making himself ridiculous.

Volate were much in vogue with the first Mozart singers; we do not use them any more as free ornaments in the middle of a piece.

But—and the average non-Latin coach seemingly ignores this—we still are free to use them occasionally in their rudimentary form, consisting only of rapidly ascending unbroken successions of untrilled notes sung on one and the same syllable. Such *volate* are called VOLATINE [tiny flights].

Here are two *volatine* for two different measures in the same aria which have an identical musical design. I hope that they will provide a better understanding of the *a piacere* vocal embroidery which one is still permitted to create. Also, they demonstrate how to sing *volatine* without distorting the rhythm.

---

see Part I, §11. I. footnote 42, p. 29, for Bernacchi see Part III, The *Musici,* Bernacchi, p. 103, for Father Martini see this Part, footnote 16, p. 43. For an exact understanding of the expression *"musico"* read Part III, Survey, p. 91.

La Serva Padrona (G. B. Pergolesi). Serpina. Aria: *Stizzoso,* ... In the *da capo* from
𝄋 : measures No. 63 and 67:

No. 63

non vi puo gio-

Original.

*ma — i vi puo gio-

Execution in style;
no not slow down.

* The word *non* is changed to *mai*
to give the *volatina* more sparkle. ** See p. 66.

No. 67

cheto e non par-

Original.

ché _____ *to e non par-

Execution in style;
do not slow down.
* See p. 74.

Tiny flights must be clear, clean and flighty, else they lose all charm and deviate into clumsy slurs.

No greenhorn of our era should try by himself to decide when and where to use a Bel Canto *volatina,* and he should keep in mind during his future career that such interpolations are not to be used for the sake of prestige, but only if the permitted liberty enhances the charm of the old composition.

c) **Mordenti:** Bel Canto's *mordente* also arises from the trill. There is no better definition of it than that of Mancini in his *Riflessioni* ... page 172 (see the previous footnote 26, p. 60).

> "The trill is composed of a true and real note vibrated equally with another note a tone higher. The *mordente* is composed of a true, real note with the throbbing of another false note a semitone **below,** and this false note must be sung more slowly and with less force than the true, real note, on which, however, both the trill as well as the *mordente* must always end."

It is needless to study this virtuosity of the throat. Nobody uses it any more.

The *mordente* [mordent, mordant] of which one generally hears nowadays is

nothing but a half-turn with downward movement [♪ notation] , of which

I have spoken in the previous chapter while explaining musical embellishments.

Sometimes it is a double half-turn  ,

sometimes a triple one  .

But just as the most perfect chain of half-turns with upward movement, called

"false trill" or inverted mordent  will never sound

like a true trill, so the most perfectly executed chain of half-turns with downward movement will never be a true *mordente*.

The "mordent" in use today has nothing in common with the true *mordente* in Bel Canto, except that both are downward movements of minor seconds.

The true *mordente* vanished with the castrated singers. I have only included it here, and given its best explanation (Mancini), because this vibration between two major semitones was a much appreciated virtuosity of the throat at the time Bel Canto was at its height.

Trills, *volate* and *mordenti* are no less musical embellishments than simple leaning notes, crush notes and composite leaning notes of all variations. Nevertheless, I have treated them as a separate group, because technically they form a completely different type of unit.

VI.   SUSTAINED NOTES

The study of sustained notes requires a well-placed voice and mastery of the vocal organs. It should be noted that, as the word **sustained** itself suggests, the voice must be perfectly supported by the breath.

It is a grave error to try to place the human voice by having the tyro exercise with sustained notes. Not only will he study without profit, but he will tire his voice.

It is a fundamental law of the old Italian school not to attempt this important and difficult part of study till after the voice of the student is well placed above the breath.

We distinguish:

a) Notes Sustained with Equal Force: These are notes that must be sung with equal force, without the slightest variation in intensity or volume and without ever losing the perfect placement of the sound above the breath. The student must be careful not to go sharp or fall flat at the end of a sustained note.[27]

---

[27] Falling flat in sustained notes is a sign either that the singer's voice is not securely placed above the breath or that the artist does not feel well. See Appendix, §1. Singing Out of Tune, p. 127.

Going sharp in sustained notes is an infallible sign that the singer is forcing his voice. Either the vocal apparatus is not as yet ripe for this phase of study or the technique is wrong. In any case, whenever a singer sings sharp he is forcing his voice, and later will regret it. See Appendix, §4. The Shaky Voice, p. 132.

b) **REPEATED NOTES:** They constitute a charming variety of the sustained notes with equal force. The voice, **without ever being interrupted,** breaks up the sustained note with a series of light and smooth repercussions of equal duration and—of course—equal force. Repeated notes should offer no difficulty to the singer who possesses a perfect *martellato,* as they present a *martellato* group to be sung on one and the same pitch.[28]

c) **MESSA DI VOCE OR SUSTENTION OF THE VOICE:** By the expressions *messa di voce* [sustention = sustentation of the voice] or, but seldom, *spianata* [suavity] we mean a sustained note or phrase attacked pianissimo and *a flauto* [flutelike] in order to be slowly and gradually reinforced to forte or fortissimo, according to the composer's instruction. The sound or sounds then follow the same line in the opposite direction, and end on pianissimo.

The musical sign for *messa di voce* [sustention of the voice] is ⊰⊱ ⊰⊱ [29]

To carry it out, the note should be attacked pianissimo almost "shut." [30] Then, without changing either the vowel or the color of the vowel (without the slightest alteration of any muscle), it is increased slowly to forte, while taking great care not to sing sharp. At fortissimo, which should **never** tax the limit of the voice, the note is cut off without releasing the breath, while being careful not to produce any shock of the glottis on detaching the note.

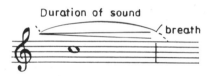

When the student has mastered the above *crescendo* = ⊰*cres.*⊱, the second part, the *decrescendo (diminuendo)* [filature] = ⊰*dim.*⊱ can be studied. The attack will be on the forte,[31] while being careful not to attack by means of a shock of the glottis. Then, without changing either the vowel or the color of the vowel (without the slightest muscular alteration) it is diminished slowly (*filato,* spun out) to pianissimo almost "shut," while taking great care not to sing flat. At pianissimo the note is detached without releasing the breath, or to say it in other words: "Keep your breath, when you stop singing!"

---

[28] See this Chapter: A: §3. I. The *Martellato* Agility, p. 68.

[29] This sign of two "forks" *(due forcelle)* was introduced into our music by the Roman priest, poet, composer, and teacher Domenico Mazzocchi (1592–1665). He also was the first, or at least one of the first, to use *p* for piano, *f* for forte, *tr* for the trill, and × for the double-sharp. Mazzocchi explains carefully all these signs—which were then strikingly new—in the introduction of his work *Partitura di Madrigalli . . . ,* and again in *Dialoghi e Sonetti,* both published Rome, 1638, by Franc. Zannetti, both now guarded in the library of Bologna's Liceo Musicale as a part of the precious documents on the early Bel Canto.

[30] See Part I, §9. The Shut Voice, p. 23.

[31] During this period of training, never on the fortissimo.

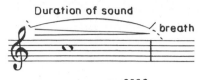

Then the complete *messa di voce* **ppp** ——<—— **cres.** ——<—— **f** ——>—— **dim.** ——>—— **ppp** must be studied on one single breath, always taking greatest care to keep the breath for a little moment after the execution of the *messa di voce*.

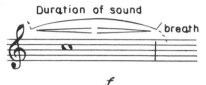

The second part, the *decrescendo* = **f** ——>—— **ppp** , is more difficult, especially on the high notes. Whoever knows how to execute a true and impeccable *messa di voce* [sustention of the voice] on the high notes can call himself a skillful artist.

I repeat: It is always necessary to take care that the vowel does not slide or shift,[32] and that the pianissimo at the end of the *decrescendo* or filature fades out without the sound losing its **complete vibration.** The latter implies that the sound has to fade out on the mixed voice, the complete voice that is both shut-in in the head and anchored in the chest. A voice must "never lose its anchorage" and deviate into one that is incomplete, into a *voce falsa* [false voice].[33] Male singers, especially tenorinos, should beware of the disqualifying, empty *"falsetto"* they love to use because this false voice comes so easy to them.

A *messa di voce,* a sustention that ends without vibration, is at its best boringly dull, but mostly it is a wail that gives pain to the hearer. Therefore, both male and female singers should be very careful.

An artist who is in the habit of attacking *a flauto* above the breath,[34] and is accustomed to changing his voice into a shut voice[35] and *vice versa* with facility and perfection, will have less difficulty than most in the filature, the spinning out (*filare*) of a sound with elegance.

d) **SUONI FILATI A FLAUTO OR ECHO NOTES:** By spun out notes in flutelike manner, by echo notes, we mean a series of notes spun out gradually on one and the same breath. Generally, the first note will already be *filato* [spun out]. Then, always on the same breath, will follow the fluted echo notes. It is none other than an exquisite variation of the *messa di voce.* But to arrive at a truly perfect production of fluted echo notes, it is necessary to **enlarge the arch of the posterior part**

---

[32] That an *a* (art) remains *a;* an *é* (fate) remains *é*; and an *è* (pen) remains *è*.

[33] Reread now most carefully Part I, §6. I. The Registers and Their Union, p. 14.

[34] See Part I, §5. Sound Attack, p. 12.

[35] See Part I, §9. The Shut Voice, p. 23.

of the mouth during the very first sustained note, without, however, having this first sustained note lose its brilliance or undergo any change of color. One is able to do so **only** after the muscles of the throat and neck have become strong and elastic through singing above the breath (*sopra il fiato*), and if the lower jaw, which has to be extremely mobile in its sockets, has been trained to obey the will.

sustained note: echoes . . . .

These echo notes may follow other graphic characters, for example,

sustained note: echoes . . . .   sustained note: echo . . . . .

and may be executed on one and the same note of the voice range, or follow any musical design.

Artistically executed echo notes have always been a sign of greatest vocal perfection.

VII.   THE *PORTAMENTI*

The smooth glide from one note to another, while making audible all the little commas[36] between them, is called a *portamento* [carrying, bridge, glide, slide, slur].

One can make a *portamento* from forte to piano, from piano to forte, from forte to forte, from piano to piano, from high notes to low, from low to high.

A *portamento* should be used only rarely, since its abuse gives the listener the impression that the artist is dragging rather than carrying one note to another. To my taste the *legato a flauto* [flutelike legato] is sweeter than the *portamento,* and experience has taught me that the more *legato a flauto* is used, the more beautiful is the singing. The public never tires of it.

The *portamento*—if not specifically indicated otherwise by the composer—is made on the syllable about to be abandoned, not on the following syllable. As a matter of fact, for a very brief instant the note of the second syllable should be heard over the first syllable. To execute this and to make audible all commas of the interval regardless of its size, the student should place mentally the second tone slowly "into" the first one while singing the latter, and sustaining it until it encloses the newcomer. The result will be the suave caress that a *portamento* is supposed to be.

Since I fear that my readers may not understand, I shall explain graphically.

---

* Breadth arc.
[36] See this Chapter: A: §2. II. The Semitones and the Chromatic Scales, p. 41.

written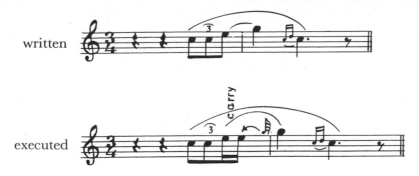

executed

Here are two exercises which show that the *portamento* should not be studied without agility. However, this most difficult part of vocal training should never be attempted before singing with words is started.

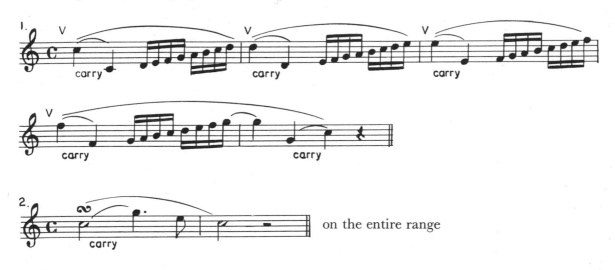

on the entire range

The *portamento* is often united with a sustention of the voice (*messa di voce*).
Here are as a sample some measures from a beautiful Neapolitan song.

Canta pe' me (Curtis).

The *portamento* when used with taste where the emotion[37] demands it, never fails to touch the listener.

§3
Non-Legato Singing

Non-legato singing should be the "offspring" of legato singing.

The old Italian school recognized only legato singing as true art. In this legato singing there was a non-legato agility (fluency), but also this was always placed above the breath.

I.   THE *MARTELLATO* AGILITY

The emission of a series of notes on one and the same breath, each note accented separately, yet without the slightest sound interruption between the single notes of the series, is called *martellare* [hammering].

The graphic signs consist of the *sforzato* (*sf*) or *sforzando* (*sfz*) signs [stress marks] > or V over each note of a series, or else dots with an arc over them.

Hammering is done by singing every note within one group on the same vowel.

a a a a
é é é é
è è è è and so forth.

Both teacher and student should remember that during a *martellato* phrase there must be neither breath nor sound interruption, and, also, that any alteration will spoil the clarity and effectiveness of this most artistic agility.

To make hammering (*martellare*) very clear, I shall try to explain it graphically:

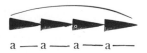

a — a — a — a —

---

[37] For this there cannot be any fixed rule.

II.   THE *PICCHETTATO* AGILITY

Notes completely detached from one another are called *picchettato* or *picchiettato* [spotted], or *staccato* [disconnected] notes.

Every *picchettato* phrase must always be executed on one and the same breath.

The graphic sign, the "staccato mark," consists of dots over the notes to be executed in *picchettato* or *staccato* fashion.

III.   THE *PICCHETTATO A FLAUTO* AGILITY

If the *picchettato* notes are not released instantly, but instead are inflected to prolong each note for a tiny instant, they are called *picchettato a flauto* [fluted *picchettato*], or *picchettato ad eco* [echo *picchettato*] notes.[38]

Of course, just as with all *martellato* and *picchettato* series, every "fluted *picchettato*" phrase must always be executed on one and the same breath.

The graphic sign is a tiny cuneiform stroke or a comma over the note itself.

These three forms of agility are easy for small, light voices, and difficult for heavy voices. Although their study gives elasticity and flexibility to the throat, **they should not be studied before the voice is securely placed above the breath.**

Their premature study could very easily misplace the voice; also, the result surely will be some kind of cackling instead of a charming vocal production.

IV.   LAUGHTER

Laughter in singing must be performed within the tonality and rhythm of the phrase or piece in which it is to be executed.

---

[38] To be distinguished from echo notes which belong to legato singing. See this Chapter: A: §2. VI. d) *Suoni Filati a Flauto* or Echo Notes, p. 65.

It is composed of ascending and descending irregular and incomplete scales. Such a "fit" of laughter—*risata*—rhythmically and musically perfect, is not attained until after much practice.

Besides this way of laughing there exists also another form which has to be performed on one single pitch. This form, too, has to be executed within the tonality and rhythm of the phrase. In my opinion, the most beautiful and perfect *risata* is the second form, the one performed on a single pitch. This form is much more graceful than that performed by scales. It is understood, of course, that it cannot be used everywhere, and it should never be used in operatic roles to depict madness.

The type of *risata* suitable for "mad" roles is very difficult. If the "laughter of madness" is to make a real impression, it requires not merely a flexible throat, but the soul of a great actor.

V.   SIGHS AND SOBS

a) **SIGHS:** Sighs are an effect of the greatest importance in lyrics. Air is inhaled while singing. .

This really cannot be studied.

In order to execute sighs, not only must one be absolute master of the vocal organ but also of one's self. I cannot explain it more simply than to say: It is necessary to acquire two souls, the grieving soul of the character represented, and the critical soul of the artist which scrupulously guides the character in his grief.

Otherwise the sighs will move the listener to nothing but laughter.

b) **SOBS:** A sob is done by a slight shake of the throat while singing, without interrupting the phrase or the rhythm.

Such sobs are used only to express a great emotion in a dramatic situation.

Sighs and sobs should never be studied by a student. They are artistic ornaments that suit only the mature artist.

§4

The Study of Solfeggi and Text Singing

The *solfeggi* are sung with the names of the notes of the fixed-Do system.

Do   re   mi   fa   sol   la   si   do.

This nomenclature was introduced in its rudimental form into music about nine hundred years ago by the Benedictine monk Guido Aretinus (*ca* 955–*ca*. 1050). He took it from the first six-verse stanza of the then most popular Latin hymn to Saint John the Baptist, composed by the deacon Paulus of Aquileia, born *ca*. 730, the son of the pagan Longobard nobleman Warnefrid. Each verse of this stanza started one tone higher in pitch than the preceding verse, so that the first syllables of the six verses together formed a scale.

HYMN TO ST. JOHN BY PAULUS DIACONUS

*UT*queant laxis	[That slackened cords
*RE*sonare fibris	May sing again
*MI*ra gestorum	The glory of thy deeds,
*FA*muli tuorum	Oh purify
*SOL*ve polluti	Thy servants' lips
*LA*bii reatum	And take away their guilt
—*Sancte Joannes.*	—Oh Holy John.]
	(Author's translation.)

In the early days of Bel Canto, in 1644, the Spanish Cistercian monk and Bishop of Vigevano (Italy), Melrosae (Juan Caramuel de Lobcowiz, 1606–1682), added by decree to Aretinus' hexachord or six-tone scale, *ut, re, mi, fa, sol, la,* a seventh note—the leading tone *si* (the English B), then called *ni.* In 1620 the blind Spanish monk Pedro de Ureña had pleaded for this subtonic *ni,* which had been used since about 1547, starting in the Flemish seven-tone solmization *"voces belgicæ."* There it had been introduced by Waelrant (1517–1595), one of the many disciples of Messer Adriano (Willaert, *ca.* 1480–1562). Messer Adriano was the founder of the Venetian school that became through the previously mentioned Giovanni Gabrieli (1557–1612) the cradle of Bel Canto.[39]

The Florentine patrician Giambattista Doni (1594–1647)—the great scientist and musicologist who reconstructed the Greek lyre, the *Lyra Barberina,* for Maffeo Barberini (Pope Urban VIII, 1623–1644)—introduced our fixed-Do system and is believed to have changed the name *ut* into *do.* Only in France the syllable *ut* is still used to express "high c."

Like most attainments of the early Bel Canto the above treated heptachord or seven-tone scale also represents a rebirth, for it is **identical** to Ptolemy's seven-tone scale which he called *diatonon syntonon,* and which he explicated in his treatise on music *Harmonikōn biblia 3* (book II, chap. 15). Ptolemy developed the *diatonon syntonon* under the influence of Egyptian and Chaldean culture out of the Pythagorean musical law that the octave be composed of five whole tone and two major semitone intervals.

The term *diatonon* meant to the ancient Greeks an interval of two whole tones plus one semitone, a fourth. When Ptolemy chose the term *diatonon syntonon* [tonic fourth] for his new octave, the meaning of the term *diatonon* changed. About 1400 years later, influenced by the Ptolemaic octave, the creative vanguards of the Bel Canto added the just mentioned subtonic B to the medieval six-tone scale. Thus

---

[39] See this Chapter: A: §1. Explanation of the Expression "Bel Canto," p. 37.

the *diatonon syntonon,* a Hellenistic rebirth of the Egyptian and Chaldean archaic seven-tone scale, became our diatonic scale, the A B C of our music.

So much for the history of our scale and its nomenclature.

In the education of any serious vocal artist the *solfeggi* form the link between the vocalized exercises for training the beginner and the music which is sung to words. They are very important, as much for the maturing of the gifted student's vocal technique into virtuosity as for the development of every student's sense of music and rhythm.

Since there are so many fine schools of *solfeggi,* it is impossible to say which *solfeggi* are to be used.

Before I start with any school of *solfeggi,* I teach my pupils, and especially my light sopranos and light tenors, to sol-fa some exercises, which they are already used to vocalizing, and which include *scalette,* semitones, and intervals of all kinds.

Here are a few of them.

The correct manner of pronouncing a syllable's end consonant only with the next syllable is indicated in parentheses on the first two of the following exercises. To train the beginner in this way is an old Italian rule for attaining beauty and freedom in singing (see Part I, §11. I. Consonants, p. 30).

Also, the following exercises indicate clearly that groups intended by a composer to be pronounced on one and the same syllable are, *in every composition,* always "tied together" in one manner or another. Tie signs must never be neglected, and both teacher and student will have to be most careful that the color of the vowel of such a group never suffers any alteration, never shifts.

Mi.....la sol mi, re.....sol fa re,   do.....fa mi do,   si.....mi re si   do.

The student should begin with this part of vocal study only after he has learned how to vocalize well—not before.

As a student's first *solfeggi* I use some of my own *solfeggi* and/or some of Concone. From these I like to pass on to those of Lamperti or Panofka, or to both, according to the voice and disposition of the student. The schools of Marchesi and Guercia are also excellent.

The result will depend not on the *solfeggi* themselves, but rather on the way the student learns to sing them.

*   *   *

In "text singing," added to the technical difficulties of artistic singing, is that of a faultless and refined enunciation of the text.

Therefore, may I suggest inserting between the study of the *solfeggi* and a student's first Italian song, the study of the famous *Metodo pratico di canto italiano per camera* [*Practical Italian Vocal Method*], by Nicola Vaccai.[40] It might be well to use some old edition where no musical misinterpretation and fewer errors have entered; the old Peters edition (Leipzig) comes with an English translation and does not distort Lesson Eight, as some others do.

These melodious exercises—starting with the mere scale and ending in the fifteenth lesson with a little *aria di bravura*—are set to most charming verses of Pietro Metastasio (1698–1782) and were thought of by Vaccai especially for his many non-Italian pupils.

They will introduce and train the student in an easy manner to the correct application of two or three vowels placed under one and the same note, which he will recurrently come across in any Italian text. Each single vowel of the two or three or—occasionally—four vowels of a group must always be articulated clearly and in a "faultless legato." To do so will come naturally to the student who, during the antecedent study period of vocalizing, has mastered the enunciation of vowels on one and the same pitch without losing his legato. If no vowel of such a group

---

[40] Nicola Vaccai (1790–1848) was a pupil of famous Giovanni Paisiello (1741–1816). Paisiello had been the last among the many pupils of Francesco Durante (1689–1755), who had been one of the best pupils of Alessandro Scarlatti (see Part I, footnote 42, first para., p. 29). Vaccai, one of the last links in the huge chain of first-class musicians from Naples' conservatories, wrote operas of lesser importance but was an outstanding voice teacher. He taught in Venice (1818–21), Trieste (1821–23), Vienna (1823), Paris (1829–31), London (1832), and Milan (1838–44).

carries an accent, the voice must rest on none; if one vowel of such a group carries an accent, this vowel—be it the first, second or third—has to dominate the others, without, however, distorting the rhythm and without the group's ever losing its obligatory legato. At the same time the student will become thoroughly acquainted with and accustomed to a correct pronunciation of a syllable's end consonant. In the *solfeggi* the only end consonant encountered was the semiconsonant "l" in *"sol."* Besides, he will learn to apply in text singing most of the embellishments he studied previously while merely vocalizing.

Vaccai's exercises should be studied by all students—professionals or dilettantes —in the manner intended by this famous teacher of a famous school, in Italian and exactly as demonstrated in the following few measures.

Vaccai
Second Lesson: First Three Measures.

Seventh Lesson: First Four Measures.

Eighth Lesson: First Four Measures.

* See p. 50.

Only when studied in this manner, which follows strictly the rules of the old Italian school, can these exercises be of real benefit to a student.

Much later, when the student starts to sing in English, he should be taught to apply the very same rules to the English text. When this is impracticable, he will have to take refuge in the short *cesura* in the manner I have demonstrated when treating the difficulties of the English end consonants in the first part of this manual (§11. I. Consonants, p. 30). When singing in public a singer so trained will bless the old masters and his own teacher who followed their rules.

§5

The Cadences and the Trill of the Finale

Bel Canto's *cadenze capricciose* [capricious cadences], referred to sometimes, until the middle of the eighteenth century, as *capricci* [capriccios, caprices], mostly were and now always are simply called *cadenze*. *Cadenze* are known throughout the English-speaking world as cadenzas, or cadences, or *points d'orgue*.

In this manual the term "cadence" has been adopted as the appropriate one. It has been used in the English translation of Tosi's treatise by Galliard (see p. 122), as well as in the English edition of Garcia's treatise (see p. 10, footnote 8), edited by his grandson the vocal teacher Albert Garcia, and published by St. John Wood, London, 1924.

Cadences are a dangerous part of Bel Canto, because they were left by the composer to the performer's discretion. This means liberty for productive fantasy, the singer becoming his own little composer. Therefore, the cadences in Bel Canto were, and still should be, personal, and every serious artist of today should be capable of composing his own cadences, as were the artists of two centuries ago.

The composing of a cadence may be compared to the creation of a leading dramatic role, when the real mime, without ever disregarding the author's intentions, crystallizes his own visions into vivid reality; or, better still, the composing of a cadence may be compared to the writing of a sonnet. Just as in these arts, the cadence also follows certain fixed rules and has to be fitted into the given frame. Within the latter and limited by the rules the performing artist may exercise, in addition to his technical and interpretative abilities, his capacity to compose.

The cadence should always be a mirror of the composition itself. It must reflect the sentiment, the musical movement, and the figured design of the composition.

It follows therefore, that each composition requires a different cadence, which must be composed so as to fit exactly into the frame of the composition. Any artist may create a variety of cadences for one and the same composition, which he may exchange at will and pleasure—*ad libitum*. But nobody can ever use one and the same cadence for two different compositions, without being ludicrous.

A singer who cannot develop his own cadences is not a complete artist. He may borrow them from artists whom he holds in great esteem, or else he may use those found in the scores of today. They have not been written by the composer himself, since the composers of the days of Bel Canto entrusted the cadences to the artist, but practical usage has sanctified them. In any case **the cadence must belong exclusively to the composition for which it was composed.**

In old times cadences were often almost endless. To suit our modern taste they should rather be too short than too long.

Cadences must remain within the tonality, or better, as old wisdom had it, faithful to the tonic (*fedele alla tonica*).

Cadences should carry the trill of the finale on the dominant, on the fifth from the bass (tonic, keynote). In 1723, Tosi[41] said: "From the laws of the old masters we learn that the trill is prepared in the cadences on the sixth from the bass so that afterwards it is heard on the fifth, because that is its place."

THE TRILL OF THE FINALE: If an artist places a cadence under the sign

preceding the finale, he must avoid the long trill, since the latter has its niche "only" in the cadence of the finale.

The musical sign ⌒ or ⌣, the Italian *corona* [crown] or *punto coronato* [crowned stop], is usually called in England a pause, in America a hold. If it stands above (⌒) or below (⌣) a rest, and especially a rest preceding the finale, the English term *pause* is the more appropriate one, because the entire accompaniment pauses while the artist executes a cadence. If it stands above a note, the American term *hold* is more precise, because the accompaniment is not suspended, and the modern artist is not permitted to improvise unrestrictedly on the note, but, in most instances, should only prolong the note for half of its value. Whoever nowadays embellishes every note crowned with a hold that he finds in an old composition, or constantly holds such notes longer than **time and a half** of their indicated value, to show the beauty of his voice and the capacity of his lungs, shows only vainglory combined with lack of musical taste.

Let us return to the important old rules concerning the trill of the finale. If an artist places the grand cadence of *bravura* [skill] on the finale, he will not fail to place a long trilled *messa di voce*[42] attacked *a flauto* on the fifth from the bass as the ending of such a cadence and immediately before finishing in style. This trill of the finale may or may not be prepared, but it must be executed on the fifth from the bass and must have a closure.

The long and trilled sustention (*messa di voce*) of the finale may be replaced by the double trill or unfolded into an arpeggio trill, and the latter may be either simple or ornate. But the artist must comprehend that arpeggio trills should be used only rarely, and that the public will never tire of the pure and long trill on the fifth.

The above mentioned rules are fundamental laws that every artist should respect for the cadences of Bel Canto. Nevertheless, while singing Bel Canto's ecclesiastic and secular music, there are cases where the trill of the cadence is not in keeping

---

[41] See this Chapter: A: §2. V. a) Trills, footnote 23, p. 56.
[42] See this Chapter: A: §2. VI. c) *Messa di Voce*, p. 64.

with our modern and entirely changed taste. This depends, of course, exclusively on the sentiment animating the old piece. Whenever the trill has to be omitted, the entire artistic development of the cadence will depend on the musical design created by the artist. The purity and the beauty of this design will be his artistic goal, and such a cadence must always be short. But if the old composition calls for the trill of the finale in the cadence, then no artist should ever forget that today, as two centuries ago, this trill must be executed on the fifth from the bass, on the dominant of the given key.

Here are five different and simple cadences which I use. Although written to fit into the Bel Canto style, they conform to our modern taste. I hope they will help in grasping this difficult part of Bel Canto.

CADENCES

1. Cadence of Finale in which a trill would not be in keeping with our modern taste:

Guglielmo Tell (G. Rossini) Matilde. *Romanza: Selva opaca, . . .*

2. Cadence of Finale which consists of a long trilled *messa di voce* with inflexions on the fifth from the bass and nothing else:

La Serva Padrona (G. B. Pergolesi) Serpina. Aria: *Stizzoso, . . .*

3. Cadence of Finale with a long trilled *messa di voce* on the fifth from the bass:

Don Pasquale (G. Donizetti) Norina. *Cavatina: So anch'io* . . .

4. Cadence of Finale with an arpeggio trill:

L'Elisir D'Amore (G. Donizetti) Adina. Aria: *Prendi;* . . .

sa - - - rai... ah.... no... sa - - rai... co- si.

5. Cadence of *bravura* on a pause sign, where the trill must be short but is not limited to the fifth from the bass:

La Traviata (G. Verdi) Violetta. Aria: pause sign over *"delizia al cor!"*

ah! .... si;   cro-ce de-li-zia, de-li-zia al cor..

cro-ce de-li-zia ah!   al ...... cor!...............

B: Styles in Bel Canto

When explaining the expression "Bel Canto" at the very beginning of Part II (p. 37), I said that it was a style of singing. Yet to be exact, Bel Canto did not consist of only one style but rather of many varied styles which were mixed and bound together in every single operatic composition.

Those styles were very refined and complicated, requiring the vocalist—or instrumentalist—to be a great artist. He had to be an excellent musician, cultured and sensitive to the utmost. Besides, the singer had to be a real virtuoso of the breath and of the throat, as well as a most skillful dramatic artist. Every sincere artist will strive hard to achieve similar mastery at all times, also today.

§1

The Recitative

Vincenzo Galilei (1533–1591), the father and chief teacher of the great Galileo Galilei (1564–1642), and Emilio del Cavaliere (*ca.* 1550–1602), the inventor (in all probability) of the *basso cifrato* [figured bass], were the very first who attempted to imitate the *parakatalogē,* the recitative of the antique Greek drama (Aristotle, Probl. 19.6 and Plutarch, 2.1140F.), in their own musical compositions.[43] When Jacopo Peri (known as "Zazzerino" [maned man], 1561–1633?), Giulio Caccini (known as "Giulio Romano," *ca.* 1545–1618), and Giuseppe Cenci (known as "Giuseppino," 15??–16??) presented from 1594 to 1599, under the sponsorship of the Florentine aristocracy, a series of *Dafne* performances, the first primitive attempts of the future opera, also the "recitative" was on its road to success.

The recitative represents the action in the opera and *opera buffa* [comic opera]; therefore the recitative is the style in Bel Canto that demands of the artist that he develop all his talents as an actor.

In the late French masterpieces the recitative is merely a declaiming recitation; it is spoken. Mozart uses both the spoken and sung recitative. In the Italian opera

---

[43] Mistakenly it was and is believed that Bel Canto's recitative was the imitation of that part of the antique Greek drama known as *melopea*. **There was no such word as melopea in classical Greek.** *Melopea* is an Italian word derived from the Greek *melopoiia*, exactly as the English *melopœia*. Even the correct Greek word *melopoiia* is not synonymous with *parakatalogē*. *Melopoiia* was the term for

   1) a making of lyric poems or music for them, and, generally, music (Aristotle, *Poet.* 6, 5sq.),
   2) the theory of music, its compositions, as opposed to its practice (Plato, *Symp.* 187D, cf. *Rep.* 404D.).

and *opera buffa* the recitative (the *recitativo cantabile*) is always sung, but it is a "spoken canto" that calls essentially for the art of a refined orator.

To sing while speaking, or, to speak while singing, or better still, to sing and speak with expression at the same time, taking care not to separate these two actions, is the complete definition of the *recitativo cantabile*.

The melody of the *recitativo cantabile* is generally written on the central notes of the artist's register, and should be performed with charm and ease.

The recitative does not permit embellishments. The only embellishments allowed are turns,[44] which may—sometimes—end a recitative.

The leaning note[45] is used in the recitative not as an embroidery but to stress the tonic accent of all words **followed by a rest,** thus bringing life into the monotony of the spoken canto.

As I explained previously, this form of leaning note is neither written nor marked, in spite of the fact that its execution is obligatory and that it would be a complete violation of style not to use it. It is sung by changing the entire first of two (or three) equal notes followed by a rest into a superior, or occasionally into an inferior, leaning note. The inferior leaning note is always more severe than the superior, which, sounding lighter, gives more charm to the spoken canto. Only a real understanding of the character that has to be portrayed and, of course, musical feeling, can here successfully decide.

Example of a recitative:

L'Elisir d'Amore (G. Donizetti) Adina. A few measures: (Every note that has to be replaced by a leaning note is written in parentheses, and the note that should be substituted is written to the left of the left parenthetical mark.)

It seems easy for the beginner to sing a recitative, but to sing it in a manner to interest the public is difficult. It is not enough to sing and articulate on the few

---

[44] See this Chapter: A: §2. IV. c) The Turn, p. 52.
[45] See this Chapter: A: §2. IV. a) The Simple Leaning Note, p. 50.

notes of its melody, and to keep in rhythm. The recitative must be recited with the "linguistic finesse" of a skillful dramatic artist, yet without ever losing rhythm or melodic purity.

And all this—plus acting—must be done to perfection.

§2

Canto Spianato or Suave Melody

The *canto spianato* is the pure legato singing of Bel Canto. Here the artist should develop the sheer beauty of tone, the equality and suavity of voice, and the ability to demonstrate his mastery of tone color.

Here is the place for faultless sustentions (*messe di voce*), filatures and echo notes (*suoni filati a flauto*),[46] for *portamenti*,[47] for trills[48] and trilled sustentions.

Here, in the pure melody the artist with rhythmic feeling will sing in *tempo rubato* [stolen tempo] of melodic line and will reveal his soul. (For those who are not familiar with the term *tempo rubato,* which is a characteristic of all Italian music, be it old or modern, classic or popular, and for the many non-Italian singers and coaches who believe, probably because *rubare* can also mean "to rob," that the execution of a phrase in *tempo rubato* asks for convulsive jerks: stolen tempo [*tempo rubato*] means the SMOOTH fluctuation of the speed within a musical phrase for reasons of emphasis. To achieve it, some notes have to be deprived of a tiny portion of their value, so that the stressed ones may be lengthened **without distorting the rhythmical flow.)**

The *canto spianato* is the part of Bel Canto that requires perfect singing technique from a flexible, free throat, in order to reveal the artist of passion, the human being created by God to sing.

To this day suavity has never ceased to be the characteristic of any genuine Italian melody.

§3

Canto Fiorito or Embellished Melody

The *canto fiorito* is highly characteristic of Bel Canto. Here, as in the suave melody, sustentions, filatures, echo notes, *portamenti*, trills and stolen tempos (*tempi rubati*) are used. But this style, as the word *fiorito* [florid] reveals, is particularly rich in all the embellishments that have been treated previously: it is the niche for all virtuosities.

---

[46] See this Chapter: A: §2. VI. Sustained Notes, p. 63.
[47] See this Chapter: A: §2. VII. The *Portamenti*, p. 66.
[48] See this Chapter: A: §2. V. a) Trills, p. 56.

It was the *canto fiorito* in Bel Canto that allowed a maximum of freedom for the artists' intuition, since most composers left the adornments to the performers' discretion.

Nearly every singer of today limits himself to execute the written or marked embroideries. He knows no better. But he should compose in some of the places marked with a pause (⌒) and, of course, in the cadences.[49]

Besides, there are scattered throughout the music of Bel Canto ornaments still in use today, which are not written or marked in our scores. They are traditional. Real artists and good teachers know them. Omitting them would only be a sign of ignorance and poor taste.

Here are two such embellished measures, just to show that such embellishments must never distort the rhythm.

Il Barbiere di Siviglia (G. Rossini) Il Conte d'Almaviva. *Cavatina: Ecco ridente ...*
      (Traditional adornments are in small notes and italics.)

Measure No. 25

Measure No. 30

---

[49] See this Chapter: A: §5. The Cadences and the Trill of the Finale, p. 75.

§4

Declamatory Singing

Declamatory singing was seldom used in Bel Canto. It excludes every agility.

This melody of passion requires perfect enunciation, powerful colors, ardent accents, sighs, unexpected changes of expression, and, sometimes, well-bridged *portamenti*.

To be a good dramatic singer, a fiery passionate soul and a **very robust vocal organ** are necessary, as well as the skill of a great actor.

This style is most dangerous for young and delicate voices, as declamatory singing easily impairs their freshness and beauty.

CHAPTER II

Other Studies

---

§1

The Study of Music and Languages

The reader will by now have grasped that in order to be able to attain real artistry, not only must one have perfect vocal and singing technique but one must also acquire a musical education suitable to the exigencies of the lyric art.

Every child knows that one cannot acquire any education without first knowing how to read and write. But there are many vocal students who have taken "singing lessons" for years and for whom the simple musical alphabet, the notes, remain hieroglyphics.

The beginning of the musical education should anticipate or at least coincide with the beginning of the education in vocal technique. There is, however, no fixed rule. But the teaching should be done in such manner as to make the pupil learn not only the fundamentals for his career as a vocal virtuoso (which means a faultless vocal and an artistic singing technique) but to help him become a critical musician under the guidance of his singing teacher.

Guided by kindness, patience, and—above all—with wisdom, the pupil cannot grasp the idea of the technique of Bel Canto without slowly acquiring the habit of controlling the purity and smoothness of sound attack, the clarity of vowels, the elegance and accurate rhythm of embellishments, the perfection of trills, and so forth. With this habit of self-control upon which every good teacher will insist, his musical taste will automatically become critical and refined.

But that is far from being enough.

In order to compose a cadence[50] one must be a bit of a composer. Only a chosen few succeed herein automatically while studying scrupulously Bel Canto's masterpieces and their multiformity. Therefore, I think it wiser not to wait for such enlightenment, but to learn how to compose correctly Bel Canto's cadences by studying the theory of music and counterpoint as a side subject.

To know how to sing in *tempo rubato* without ever distorting the rhythm, one must have a very educated and perfect innate sense of rhythm. May I advise every zealous student of singing with deficiency in this most important sense to study the

---

[50] See this Part, Chapter I: A: §5. The Cadences and the Trill of the Finale, p. 75.

piano for a while; it will be of great help. Some parents dedicate their child at a very early age to a singing career. May I suggest that such a child study the violin, because through this instrument the youthful ear will grow very sensitive to purity of pitch and to quality of tone. It would be wise to choose a violinist from a symphony orchestra as the little singer's first violin teacher.[51]

Besides acquiring a profound general music education, every singer should endeavor to cultivate his native tongue in its purest structure and richest linguistic forms. He should become familiar with the masterpieces of world literature, both prose and poetry. It surely belongs to the many duties of the teacher of an aspiring artist, an "I-want-to-be-an-artist," also to educate the linguistic taste of the latter and to inspire him to read mankind's best books.

Foreign languages, likewise, must not be neglected. Each language should be studied with a person of educated diction, and who is a native of the very heart of the respective country. Thus, French should be taken up with a Parisian and not, for example, with someone from Alsace-Lorraine; pure Italian, *"lingua toscana in bocca romana"* [Tuscan idiom with the Roman accent], should be studied with a Roman or a Tuscan and not with a Southern Italian or one from the Trentino. Such sagacity in the choice of a language teacher should be applied without exception for the study of each language, for any dialect, and for any argot as well, because having the purest accent of any idiom wherein one wishes to sing will ease the road that leads to a first-class singing career.

§2
The Study of Expression

Any work of art that lacks expression and idea ceases to be art and becomes a dead thing. This is also true of singing.

Singing may be perfect in technique, but if the melody lacks expression it will not touch the heart of the listener.

To have the power of expression in addition to perfect vocal technique, above all one must have the power to **feel.** If the artist desires to touch his listener, he himself must be profoundly moved by what he wishes to express, or at least must be capable of a vivid understanding of the sentiments he is interpreting. This attitude requires a high state of natural sensibility which mere study will never furnish, but which can be guided and regulated through study.

In order to become familiar with an accent of passion, a student must feel it profoundly and sincerely. Then he must concentrate on a severe analysis of all the sensations he himself undergoes during this emotion. It is only by such procedure that he will be able to reproduce at any time the exact portrait of the emotion he wishes to communicate to his audience.

May I advise all young singers to analyze and criticize the sensations of their

---

[51] See Appendix, §1, Singing Out of Tune, second para., p. 127.

everyday life. By such analysis and self-criticism not merely the interpreter in them will mature, but their thoughts will become ennobled in every sense of the word.

Every being has—according to his temperament, his position in society, his age, and so forth—his own particular manner of feeling and expressing himself. The artist must have the power of eliminating his personal identity and of projecting himself completely into the character of the person whom he wishes to represent. Yet he should never fail to guide critically this being created by his soul, even in the most vivid transports of passion. Only such a personage will have real life.

To achieve this difficult but most important goal, I advise every student of dramatics to do as the successful mime does—**to forget his own ego,** and to create and elaborate in his imagination the character he wishes to impersonate. Then the student must permit this character to gesticulate and sing under the severest criticism of his inner eye. Only thus will the young mime slowly perfect himself, and the day will arrive when he will be able to express the most vivid passion without losing for an instant the cool self-control of the great interpreter.

On the concert stage no acting is permitted. It spoils the appearance to gesticulate with body, arms, or even only with hands. It is important to stand straight and free as in a singing lesson, and to transmit to the audience the creation of the composer, reflected through one's own soul, with the voice and the voice alone.

§3
The Application of the Various Timbres

The lyric as well as the dramatic artist who has complete control of his entire vocal apparatus never fails to be master of all the timbres needed to give life to a character. He can sing and/or speak brightly or darkly, sonorously or colorlessly, lovingly or loathingly, imploringly or commandingly. In short, he can give each word its proper shade.

However, the selection of the color must by no means depend on the literal sense of the words, but on the sentiment of the phrase. There is no set rule. It is artistic feeling which decides. In general, it can be said that pain darkens the voice to the point of inaudibility; that joy is produced by vivid and brilliant colors; that laughter has a metallic timbre; that one weeps in lusterless desolation; that a threat should show an open-ringing voice; and so on in all the combinations, *ad infinitum*.

To the "born-artist" who also has strong vocal organs and a loose and free throat, the right color comes automatically. But in this play of colors the audience must always hear every word of the text.

******

Sing my young friends, sing stoutheartedly!

IN BOCCA AL LUPO! [Break-a-leg!]

Part III

THE CASTRATED SINGERS

and Their Role in Bel Canto

Not long ago humanity has closed the gates
    Behind the last unhappy lark;
Their joyous trills, their hidden tears have ceased to flow
    And fill with shame the fair and free.
OH, MAY NO MAN IN BRAZEN LUST FOR MIGHT OR GOLD
    DISGRACE AGAIN A GIFTED CHILD!

Survey

Music has the power to gladden mankind
—*Aristotle*

Let us look far back into history and follow the evolution of the castrated singers on their long, tear-filled road from lowliness and degradation to glory and artistic leadership of immortal fame.

The castrated singers had their origin where castration had its origin—in the brains of evil despots. It is mostly stated, especially in the English literature dealing with this subject, that mankind's very first castrated singer appeared in 1601 and was an Italian, to be precise, *padre* Giovanni Rossi, or as the English music historian Charles Burney (1726–1814) calls him, Father Girolamo Rossini. But, as the following pages clearly prove, the historical facts are entirely different.

According to Clearcus, disciple of Aristotle, castration started in Asia, more precisely in Media (*Anthenaeus, Deipnosophistarum sive Coenae Sapientium* [Banquets of the Scholars]). And it is well known that the Pharaohs of ancient Egypt already used this torment as punishment, just as Hitler did in our day and for similar reasons. Moses strictly forbade it to his people, but Queen Semiramis kept an entire army of eunuchs at her court, selecting from them the paramours and singers for her lustful orgies.

The Romans learned to emasculate from the Greeks, who were in antiquity the most requested surgeons for this operation. Both Romans and Greeks castrated boys before puberty to form singers with **voices higher and brighter than male voices, which at the same time were more powerful than any female voice ever can be—"female voices in male chests."**[1] The Arabs did the same thing long before Mohammed and for the same reason; it was only after Mohammed that the entire Moslem world took up the lawful emasculation of men as chaperones for the countless slave concubines in the harems. Even the Hottentots deep in Africa castrated the vocalists of their wild, primitive rituals.

Just as Greece had inherited many cults from Asia and Egypt, thus ancient Rome, and later the powerful medieval popes, absorbed willingly many oriental ways of thinking and doing, many cruel customs and barbaric cults, not merely the crime of depriving men of their manhood.

The castrated singers so well known to antiquity appeared in the Catholic world, to be precise in the service of the popes, at the end of the twelfth century (Matteo

---

[1] To comprehend the enormous range and power of their voices, see the last para. of the Survey, p. 98 and the second para. of The *Musici*, p. 100.

Fornari, *Narrazione istorica . . . della Pontificia Cappella . . . col Catalogo dei Cantori*[2]). The Italian historian Fantoni, in his *Storia universale del canto,* 1873, quotes a canonist of this epoch: "*Olim cantorum ordo non ex eunuchis ut hodie fit*" ["Once the class of singers did not consist of eunuchs, as it does today"]. In 1441 the pontifical records no longer mention the presence of boys, but the use of basses, tenors and eunuchs. A papal bull of Pope Sixtus the Fifth (1585–1590) addressed to the Apostolic Nuncio of Spain reveals that for *a long time* the *castrati* had been used as church singers throughout all Italy. Those church singers were called contemptuously *falsetti,* or, worse, *evirati* [the emasculated ones, geldings]—in France *châtrés* [geldings] or *incommodés* [the invalids]. The latter name was given to them by the *Précieuses* under Louis XIII (1601–1643). The Germans used the very insulting word *Kapaune* [capons, fattened castrated cocks].

The canons of the cruel Middle Ages banished all women's voices from the church, favoring the very unchristian but inexpensive custom of using instead these mercilessly mutilated males. Not only this; the medieval Church anathematized all women who sang in public, and thus nearly everywhere the women, sopranos and contraltos, were supplanted by the *falsetti,* by *sopranisti* [sopranists] and *contraltisti* [contraltists], as they were called. Not until the sixteenth century did the female voice re-enter "sporadically" Italy's secular singing. The first really good one was Vittoria Archilei, born—oh irony—in Rome, *ca.* 1565. Other Italian female artists of this era were *la bella Adriana* (Adriana Basile, 15??–16??) and her gifted daughter Leonora Baroni,[3] Francesca Caccini, soprano, famous composer and poetess born in 1588,[4] her three sisters, and a few more.

The papacy did not sanction this. Pope Paul IV (1555–1559)—the very same pope who decreed that no married man was to be admitted as a singer to the Pontifical Chapel,[5] who chased Palestrina[6] from his employment there on July 30, 1955, only because he was married and had to feed a family—again banished all

---

[2] This treatise, written in the eighteenth century and containing a complete catalogue of the *castrati* in pontifical service back to the twelfth century, was guarded in the library of Bologna's academy of music, the famous Liceo Musicale. Mysteriously it got lost.

[3] Milton's Leonora of his famous Latin epigram *Ad Leonoram Romae canetem* (1638).

[4] Francesca Caccini, mostly called by her nickname "Cecchina" [little chatterbox], was the best pupil of her father, Giulio Caccini, know as "Giulio Romano," *ca.* 1545–1618, a singer, flutist, teacher and great composer. Giulio Romano belonged to the daring trio which, in 1594, introduced the musical drama into our culture, as has been reported in Part II, Chapter I: B: §1. The Recitative, p. 80. Cecchina was the first woman who composed with real success; her "sing-ballet" *La liberazione di Ruggiero dall' Isola d'Alcina* (1625) was famous. Much literature on both father and daughter Caccini is available. Any audience will enjoy Francesca Caccini's delicate little song *Dove io credea le mie speranze vere,* G. Ricordi. Recommended as a delightful encore for a man's concert repertory is Giulio Caccini's *Amarilli,* G. Ricordi. After nearly four hundred years the little love song has not lost any of its charm.

[5] See Part II, Chapter I: A: §1. Explanation of the Expression "Bel Canto," footnote 2, p. 37.

women's voices, this time forever, from St. Peter's, Rome. He also decreed several times during his pontificate that they should be replaced in all churches and in all secular singing by *evirati*. Pope Innocent XI (1676–1689), "Papa Minga" [I refuse],[7] in a Brief, even forbade women to take singing lessons from men (Pastor's *History of the Popes,* 1885). Still today the Pontifical Church does not admit the female voice. In St. Peter's only men and boys may sing to the praise of the Lord. The Sistine Choir, the personal *a cappella* choir of the pope, consists normally of ten tenors, eight basses and twelve *falsettisti*. (This expression indicates male voices that have been trained to sing in a falsetto voice above the range of the natural male voice[8] without the help of castration. Maybe it would be clearer if I added: a *falsettista* is no more than a most efficiently trained countertenor or male alto. Unfortunately, even the best of these voices lack beauty.[N6]) To these thirty very

---

[6] Palestrina, whose real name was Giovanni Pierluigi, was born in Palestrina near Rome in 1529 (not 1525) in a brick house that still greets the exploring tourist. He died in Rome in February 1594 (not 1593) and was buried in the *Cappella nuova* [New Chapel] of St. Peter's, which is probably today's Gregorian Chapel. He started his studies and career when a boy of twelve as a *puer cantus* [boy singer] in the chapel of the Liberian Basilica of Saint Mary Major in Rome. It is impossible to outline with only a few strokes the extraordinary importance of this genius, who with his Mass for six voices *Papae Marcelli,* written for and sung at the Council of Trent (1545–1563) during its last session (1562/63), saved music from being ousted by the Council from all churches because of the extremely low criterion of the musical texts and the deafening accompaniments that had become "noisy stutter." (Previously, in March, 1561, the music loving Prince Rodolfo di Carpi, Cardinal Carpi, had sent the best pontifical singer, the "*castratus* Simon Perusinus" [see this Part, footnote 17, p. 95] with eight other reliable pontifical vocalists to the Council of Trent to save the situation, but without favorable result). It is also impossible to narrate briefly all the hardships a cruel era brought upon the composer of a *Stabat Mater,* which is of such rare beauty that for more than three hundred and fifty years it has been performed on Palm Sundays by the Pope's Chapel. It is the very same *Stabat Mater* from which Wagner, in deep admiration, took the introductory chords for the evocation of "Good Friday" in *Parsifal,* changing only the foremost chord from major to minor. Much literature on Palestrina, written by outstanding men, is readily available. It would be worth while reading various biographies of him. Not only will the importance of Palestrina become clearer, but the reader—and especially the fortunate American who knows no chains—will understand more easily a period when the majority of the people were completely at the mercy of the men in power, when the average man had no rights (just think about the sufferings of Galileo Galilei), when there was no freedom for him—and, for the most part, no food either.

[7] Once a sopranist presented a petition to "Papa Minga" asking to be allowed to marry, because, as he explained, he was a male; whereupon the Pope wrote on the margin: "*Che si castri meglio!*" ["That he be better castrated!"] (Blondeau, *Histoire de la musique moderne,* Paris, 1847).

[8] See Part I, Fig. 6—Table of Registers, Complete Picture of Male Voices in Their Two Registers, p. 15.

[N6] The only male who can be trained "successfully" to sing in the female range with a complete male volume is the Negro tenorino (light tenor), because he often possesses by

cultured adult singers—coming more or less from the Pontifical University of Sacred Music (Pontificio Istituto di Musica Sacra)—are added as many boy singers as are needed from the enormous Scuola Pia [Holy School]. Those boys, sopranos and altos, are no dilettantes, they are the best boy singers in the world. Before entering the pontifical Scuola Pia, each young singer is carefully chosen from the best of the many choir schools which the Catholic Church runs—mostly from the School for Singers of the Holy Saviour in Lauro (Schola Cantorum di S. Salvatore in Lauro), in Rome. This school was founded by the pope in 1868 especially for boy singers; it has furnished since its foundation the most efficient adult ecclesiastical singers of our era. *There are no castrated singers in today's occidental Christian world;* the last castrated opera star, Velluti,[9] died in 1861; the last castrated virtuoso, Domenico Mustafà "Permanent Director of the Pontifical Chapel,"[10] died in 1912. He is the same Mustafà whose art in 1892 threw Paris into a growing state of ecstasy. He was then sixty-three years old. The occidental world's very last castrated singer, *Monsignore* Alessandro Moreschi,[11] died in Rome in 1922, and his voice is the only *castrato* voice that has been recorded. May the United Nations grow strong enough to be able to stop the crime of castration, which is still flourishing in Asia[12] and Africa, where plenty of boys are mutilated—and not for the sake of any art.

Since the Middle Ages, not only the pope but also various emperors, kings, dukes, bishops, patriarchs—in short all sovereigns, big or small, secular or ecclesiastical, asked for falsetti for their church choirs as well as for their vicious banquets and drinking bouts. These *falsetti* belonged to the court staff as did the unhappy

---

nature—without the help of castration—in addition to his male chest and falsetto voices also a real head voice which can be awakened with all its female characteristics. With appropriate training such a voice can, of course, be developed into a voice of no less power and charm than the voice of a castrated virtuoso. For a clear understanding of this footnote and its importance, read the last para. of this Survey and study most carefully Part I, §6. I. The Registers and Their Union, p. 14 and its Table of Registers.

[9] For his biography see this Part, The *Musici*, Velluti, p. 122.

[10] For his biography see this Part, The *Musici*, Mustafà, p. 116, for Pontifical Chapel = Apostolic Chapel see Part II, Chapter I: A: §1. footnote 2, p. 37.

[11] For his biography see this Part, The *Musici*, Moreschi, p. 116.

[12] Castration was outlawed in China in 1912 after having ravaged that country for over three thousand years. The gates then opened for the poor Chinese slave eunuchs, who now, driven by hunger, formed gangs and roamed through the country, where they were hated, feared and scouted. China is a vast country with obsolete and inadequate communications; in 1935, the outlawing of castration was still in numerous remote districts somewhat ineffective, and many eunuchs in their teens and even younger were to be seen. They were completely illiterate and lived in indescribable filth and misery. In 1958, I taught a Chinese castrated singer. He called himself an "eunuch soprano," although he was no sopranist but a contraltist. He was twenty-five years old, was a refined and cultured man, but his voice was edgy and far from being pleasing. In 1959, I helped another Chinese "eunuch soprano." This time it was a sopranist, and his voice was even more offensive.

jesters and whipped hunchbacks. Like them the *evirati* were medieval lackeys—lowly slaves and nothing more. Some German sovereigns "consumed" so many *Kapaune* that, besides importing them, they made their own by including among their court staff a special surgeon to perform this operation. These surgeons came mostly from the University of Bologna, which was the center of science in the Middle Ages and in the Renaissance, just as Greece had been such a center in antiquity.

Up to the end of the sixteenth century nearly all *falsetti* came from cruel and hungry Spain. They were called contemptuously *ultramontani*[13] [ultramontane] ever since they had followed Pope Gregory XI when he returned to Rome from Avignon in 1377; they were not well received in Rome and were hated by most of the Italian singers with whom they were united in the Collegio dei Cappellani Cantori Pontificii [College of the Pontifical Chanter Chaplains[14]], the famous papal body of singers and composers which was founded at that time. Outstanding in the late Spanish group of evirated singers was *Don* Francesco Soto da Langa (not—as mostly stated—Sorto), 1539–1619, a sopranist, a composer, and a teacher at the Sistine Chapel. He died "Dean (*decano*) of the Apostolic Chapel" after having served there fifty-seven years. The last exponent of this group was Giovanni de Sanctos, who died in Rome in 1625 (Matteo Fornari, *Narrazione istorica* . . .[15]). When Orlandus de Lassus (1520–1594) was called to the Bavarian court in 1566 as a tenor, of the six *Kapaune* belonging to the court chapel[16] *none was an Italian*. They lived wretchedly in the *Gesindestube* [servants' hall], had to obey the orders of a town crier, their autocratic guardian, and were far from being stars.

Slowly the situation changed.

The first "Italian" sopranist in papal service whose status has been traced incontestably was Simon Perusinus, who from 1561 to 1563 was the leader of the singers at the Council of Trent, as pointed out previously.[17] The first "Italian" contraltist

---

[13] Later this disdainful and hostile term was used as an insult for the entire party upholding papal supremacy. To this day Italy's anti-papal party calls the papal party *ultramontani*.

[14] It is erroneous to believe that the word "chaplain" refers exclusively to a clergyman who is officially attached to the army or navy. *A chaplain is a clergyman with many different functions and obligations.* He may be attached to some public institution, or to the household of a wealthy family and may be in charge of instructing and educating the children of the family, or he may be attached to a court, and so forth. The word "chaplain" is also used to indicate a lay person in the service of the church. Attached to the Pope's Chapel are various grades of chaplains, and generally the papal singers rank as "common chaplains," to whom in 1907 Pope Pius X confirmed the title of *Monsignore*.
The word "chanter" signifies here an ecclesiastical singer.

[15] The previously mentioned treatise that vanished from Bologna's precious library. See this Part, footnote 2, p. 92.

[16] See Part II, Chapter I: A: §1. Explanation of the Expression "Bel Canto," footnote 2, p. 37.

[17] Simon Perusinus was the ecclesiastical name of Simone Bartolini, who was known

of the Pontifical Chapel was in 1580 the twenty year old Gian Luca Conforti. He is the same who in 1592 reintroduced the trill into our music.[18] The first falsetto, so highly appreciated that he was ennobled by Pope Urban VIII (1623–1644) to the rank of *knight of the Militia of Jesus Christ,* was *Don* Soto's (see p. 95) favorite, the Italian sopranist Loreto Vittorj da Spoleti (*ca.* 1588–1670), an opera and church singer, a teacher, a composer, and a poet.[19] Before entering into pontifical service he had been singing at the court of the Medici, the sovereigns of Tuscany. Besides, *Cav.*[19] Vittorj was the first *falsetto* to teach royalty, having become the Swedish Queen Christina's voice teacher in Rome.

Two other early Italian *castrati* who helped to prepare the path of the *castrati* for world fame were the sopranist and composer Francesco Severi Perugino (*ca.* 1556–1630) and the Roman contraltist Stefano Landi (*ca.* 1590-*ca.* 1655). Both spent all their lives in the service of the Church. Landi composed *Sant' Alessio,* a sacred drama to the libretto of his protector, Prince Giulio Rospigliosi, the later Pope Clement IX (1667–1669); it was given with the greatest pomp in 1634 for the inauguration of the Barberini theater.[20]

Hereafter, exploited by foreign oppressors, under which Naples and Southern Italy pined away in misery, and, moreover, morally encouraged by a clergy greatly in need of *falsetti* for its churches, the mean but lucrative business of boy emasculation became centered completely in Italy. The world centers for castration in the seventeenth century and thereafter were Naples and the city of Legge in Apulia. In the eighteenth century more than a thousand boys were castrated every year in Naples alone. Of course, most of them could not succeed as singers. The gifted ones

---

also as *"l'evirato Perugino"* ["the eunuch of Perugia"]. See this Part, footnote 6. p. 93. Also of the other eight pontifical singers at the Council four were *castrati* (Matteo Fornari, *Narrazione istorica* . . . ; see this Part, footnote 15). The correct names of all of them, but not their status, are to be found in *Osservazioni per ben regolare il coro* . . . , pages 166 and 167, by Adami da Bolsena (a pontifical sopranist from the Upper Latium, known also as Adami da Volterra, 1663–1742), Rome, 1711, published by Antonio de' Rossi. Because *Osservazioni* . . . is an extremely rare book and **no other complete and reliable list of the singers at the Council of Trent exists,** I enumerate below all eight correct names to help chronologists interested in this particular part of history: Giovanni Antonio Latini da Benevento (Italian); Giovanni Luigi de Vescovi (Neapolitan); Mattia Albo di Fuligno (Italian); Pietro Scorteccio d'Arezzo (Italian); Francesco Bustamante (Spaniard); Luigi Conginguo Gisonen (probably a Spaniard from Girone [Gerona] or a Frenchman from Gisors); Bartolomeo le Cont (Frenchman); Francesco Druda (Frenchman).

[18] For his biography see this Part, The *Musici,* Conforti, p. 106.

[19] Vittorj is often misspelled as Vittori, or erroneously referred to as Lorenzo Vettori, or as born in 1604.

Cav. is the abbreviation for *cavaliere* [knight].

[20] The Barberini theater was built into the Barberini palace by Cardinal Francesco Barberini, a nephew of the refined musician Maffeo Barberini, the extremely broad-minded Pope Urban VIII (1623–1644), for whom Doni (see Part II, Chapter I: A: §4. The Study of *Solfeggi,* p. 71) reconstructed the Greek lyre. Three thousand spectators could be seated in this theater.

filled—when lucky—first the many conservatories of Italy (Naples for a while had four), then the upper and lower ranks of Europe's music world; the less fortunate were absorbed by the Italian clergy in one way or the other. **The Italian Catholic Church never let them perish, never humiliated them, but always found a niche for each of them, into which somehow he could fit.**

The Italian with his open throat and melodious speech who from early childhood had been dedicated by his parents to singing, and who had been—as we would call it—a child prodigy, could only mature into a sincere artist. Without infamous castration before mutation,[21] he would have matured after mutation into a cultured and beautiful tenor or bass; even should he have lost his voice during mutation, he always would have been a good and dependable musician. These singers made, of course, by far the best *falsetti*. Therefore we see Italian *falsetti* at the end of the seventeenth century in all theaters, in all Catholic churches, and at all courts. They had caressing voices, voices which charmed and enchanted in a magic way; they were extremely gifted; they had been, with a few exceptions, most carefully sheltered,[22] provided for, and educated in Italy's best conservatories;[23]

---

[21] See this Part, The *Musici,* second para., p. 100.

[22] For instance: their dormitories in the conservatories were heated, while the dormitories of the other students were not, which seems to have greatly impressed the fourteen year old Mozart (1756–1791) while sojourning in Venice and Bologna during his famous Italian tour.

[23] The word *conservatorio* [conservatory] comes from *conservare* [to keep]. It was a place where needy children and poor orphans were kept and educated, and a conservatory was originally merely an orphan asylum. Yet, very soon the word changed its meaning, because of the intensive musical education which was given there, since that is what the Southern Italian was and is gifted for. Naples alone had three, and for a while four conservatories—Madonna di Loreto, Santo Onofrio a Capuana, Poveri di Gesú Cristo, and Santa Maria della Pietà dei Turchini. The first, Madonna di Loreto [Virgin Mary of Loreto], was established in 1537. Its founder was Father Giovanni di Tapia, a Spanish priest and musician. Indefatigably he had gone begging from town to town for nine years, until, after adding all his own property, he had the funds for the conservatory's foundation. This benefactor of Italian youth lies buried in the school's church. Madonna di Loreto, also called San Loreto or S. M. Loreto, sheltered 300–400 poor boys, to whom the best education was given. They studied composition, all instruments, voice, Italian, Latin, French, speech, dramatics, history, and so forth. All subjects were taught by the best teachers of the time. Santo Onofrio [Saint Onuphrius], another of the four conservatories just enumerated, became one of the most famous music schools which ever existed, with the greatest Italian musicians as teachers. Here are a few of its teachers for voice and composition: Scarlatti, Gizzi, Porpora, Durante, Leo, Hasse, and Fagò. The same applies for Bologna, Venice, and so forth.

Also Germany, with its many autonomous sovereigns, had conservatories for orphans and poor children attached to the various court chapels (see Part II, Chapter I: A: §1. footnote 2, p. 37). Some of them had a special division for *Kapaune*. Burney, in 1772, reports on the art school which was attached to the summer castle of the Duke of Württemberg, and which carried the necessary surgeons from Bologna on its staff and

they had studied from ten to twelve years, day after day, from dawn to dusk under the most expert teachers of their poor but very artistic homeland, and those teachers, very often *falsetti* themselves, had loved teaching them. Under their guidance and influence these poor mutilated boys had grown into most productive and ambitious artists themselves, into good composers, and **into vocal artists and vocal teachers such as the world had never had before.**

Thus we see that the status of the *falsetti* changed completely, changed from lowliness and servility into a spoiled stardom. With such evolution the humiliating name *falsetto* and the worse one *evirato* had changed into *musico* or *musicus*[24] for reasons of courtesy as well as for antonomasia (*musicus* means connoisseur of music).

One of the first *musici* who sang outside Italy was Marc' Antonio Pasqualini (1614–1691). This pontifical sopranist was called to Paris as an opera singer and sang there on the stage for more than seventeen years.

The first real "star" *musico* to be called from one European court to another and be overloaded with honors and gold was the sopranist Baldassare Ferri (1610–1680).[25] He was a forerunner and one of the best singers in this long chain of Bel Canto's vocal virtuosi.

"Vocal virtuosi": this name seems correct if we consider that many a sopranist had a range of more or less four octaves, from B or even A—vibrations not quite 108.75 (our international pitch), to a^3 (a above the female high c), sometimes even to b^3—vibrations not quite 1953 (our international pitch). For a thorough understanding of the huge *castrato* range, verify these and the following vibrations in Part I, Fig. 6—Table of Registers. In Aldovrandini's (1675–1707) opera *Cesare in Alessandria* (1700) the sopranist had to perform on one and the same breath a scale of more than two octaves and back, ending it hereafter with an embellishment; in Scarlatti's *Il canto del rossignolo* the singer—*castrato* or not—was supposed to perform in *largo assai* a clean scale of trills over the interval from a^1—vibrations not quite 435 (our international pitch), to f^2—vibrations not quite 690.5 (our international pitch). How many of our living "stars" can do that? "Vocal virtuosi": this name

---

payroll. He also narrates how poorly the young *Kapaune* sang—so badly that seldom could any of them ever be used as a singer. The Duke did not order a niche for these poor "wretches by His Majesty's Command." They were kicked into hunger, disdain, and misery as soon as they were useless to him, because the German Duke had neither the heart nor the dignity of the Italian Church. His ancestors, too, were lacking in human feeling. It is reported that in 1658 Duke Eberhard III (1628–1674) complained about the bad singing of his *Kapaune;* he, also, kicked them out, and ordered new ones to be "delivered" to his castle. The Habsburgs in Vienna were no cruel sovereigns. Nevertheless, young Haydn scarcely escaped the feared *Kapaunenmühle* [mill for capons].

[24] To translate *musico* by "musician," and vice versa, would be entirely wrong, because since the evolution of the castrati into stardom the Italian word *musico* and the Latin word *musicus* have been used to signify a castrated singer. The only correct translation of "musician" into Italian is *musicista*.

[25] For his biography see this Part, The *Musici*, Ferri, p. 113.

becomes insufficient if we consider that a star *musico* was able to perform a most perfect *messa di voce* from *pp* to *ff* and back again to a *filo di voce*—strong, smooth, and thin as a silk thread—on a note far above high c (soprano clef [ ] not tenor clef [ ]), and that he did so *with the ease and volume of a Caruso* doing the same thing, only . . . Caruso's *messe di voce* were about *two* octaves lower.[N7] If further we consider that a *musico* had been trained and was master of the art of improvising complicated cadences in front of an audience without ever losing the key or the frame of the composition, we will understand that the very artistic minded Catholic clergy in its deep devotion to its Church longed for these artists, favored them because they opened the hearts to emotions normally unknown to men. Who did not? Even Napoleon I wept when Crescentini[26] sang *Ombra adorata aspetta* and knighted him as a tribute to his artistry—and Napoleon surely was not a melomane.

[N7] TO THE NEGRO LIGHT TENOR: reread now this Part, footnote N6, p. 93.
[26] For his biography see this Part, The *Musici*, Crescentini, p. 107.

The Musici

I felt a delight unknown to me ever before . . .
—*Goethe*

There has been much ugly talk by serious men concerning the *musici*. Some believe that all of them suffered from bad temper; according to some they were "vicious parasites"; according to others, eunuchs were too tall for the opera stage—"six feet and over"; some saw in them "fat hams with disgusting bellies"; "they were cowards." Some writers—J. J. Rousseau in a fit of envy and in our century de Martini of the Paris conservatory—are positive that they lost their voices at an early age—yes, to some their unnatural voices sounded "disgusting" (F. G. Becker, *Zur Geschichte der Castraten,* Mainz, 1828).

The truth about them is that they were very gifted unfortunates, because a castrated boy usually grows into a being with sexual desires of a male, without being a male. It happens especially if the operation is executed in the manner that was usually adopted in Italy. This means that of the four types of operations the surgeon performed the smallest type which accomplished the purpose—the prevention of mutation. While the thorax of the castrated boy developed into the thorax of a male, his vocal organs did not lose boyhood's female characteristics. The cartilages of the larynx and especially the thyroid cartilage did not assume masculine shape, nor did they harden. Also the fibres and the muscles of the vocal organs—primary as well as secondary—kept the female flexibility, a characteristic of boyhood. Therefore, the emasculated adult, with his female vocal apparatus and his male thorax, had a voice much higher and brighter than the best tenor, sometimes even higher than most of our sopranos.[27] The support of such a voice in both its male and female ranges by strong male lungs resulted in an ample voice far more powerful in its upper register than any female voice can ever be, no matter how well it is trained. It is understood, of course, that the necessary operation, aiming exclusively at the prevention of mutation, had to be performed at a very early age, before any visible or invisible symptoms of puberty appeared, consequently during childhood. This is the reason that most victims of this criminal practice were less than eight years of age, a fact which aggravates the infamy of such mutilations.

The *musici* were very much courted by the grand ladies of bygone days, and by powerful men too. They had many love affairs in an aristocracy which idolized them. They were often openly ridiculed, often humiliated with perverse offers from

---

[27] See this Part, the last chapter of the Survey, p. 98.

the men they served, and were sometimes persecuted by them for reasons of jealousy. The fine sopranist—not contraltist, as often stated—Siface (Giovanni Francesco Grossi), who had an excellent reputation, was even murdered in 1697 by hired assassins to satisfy the superiority complex of an overbearing yet most cowardly man of noble birth. Balzac has painted the tragedy of their lives in his interesting novel *Sarrasine*.

Every era has some perversities which appear despicable to the following one, and there is surely no reason to treat disdainfully the *musici* who, with some few exceptions, succeeded in living in very vicious times without losing their integrity. Nor is there any reason to belittle these artists who contributed so greatly to our culture, and it is surely unjust to blame parents who lived in extreme poverty for longing to open a brighter future to a beloved, gifted son. The guilt rests entirely with the society that created them and with those who used their might to order such mutilation *ad honorem Dei* [to the honor of the Lord]. These words are to be found in a special Brief of Pope Clement VIII of the year 1600.

The following pages give an alphabetical list of only a very few of the best or most interesting *musici* of fame, not their complete roll, since the latter would fill endless pages.

The biographies will not be sketched in the usual manner, containing all data from the cradle to the grave, because this information may be found for most of the *musici* in any good dictionary of musicians, once the correct list is at hand.

Instead, I will try to bring the *musici* to life by using, besides historical facts, some of the many cherished anecdotes still told in their homeland, which illuminate their good and noble traits as well as their weaknesses and faults. Thus the reader will come to understand that their souls were not different from the souls of our artists. At times they were kind, and at others selfish; at times real artists, at other instances vainglorious fools—just as all of us are—but—many of them were more often kind than selfish. Only Caruso had a heart for struggling fellow singers,[28] as did Ferri, Pistocchi, Bernacchi, Marchesi, Tosi, Crescentini, and many other *musici*. Perhaps this was because Caruso, too, came from Italy's peaceful slums, filled with love songs and contentment.

The *musici* were not merely the best singers and vocal teachers. Many of them were highly thought of as composers too. They did not need coaches to drub every single beat into them as do some of the "stars" of our day. **They were real creative artists in every sense of the word;** who loves music owes them esteem.

Some were "oversized and fat"—Senesino (Francesco Bernardi) or Niccolini; some were "oversized and too thin"—Pacchierotti or Farinelli "with the arms and legs of a spider," but Cusanino was "tall, handsome, majestic," while the German-born Porporino was "graceful and coquettish as the most graceful tiny gentlewoman

---

[28] The American-born tenor *Kammersänger* [singer of the imperial chapel] Piccaver, the pride of Vienna's opera house in its golden days, and the Italian baritone and rare interpreter *Comm.* Borghese would never have become famous singers without Caruso's help.

can be" (President de Brosses, *Lettres sur l'Italie,* 1739, published posthumously 1799). Senesino (Andrea Martini) was "loved by all for the adorable charm of his looks and for the decency of his ways," and there was Fontana, nicknamed "Farfallino" [small Mr. Butterfly = volatile man], who never failed to live up to his nickname. Nature played with them, as nature plays with all creatures and all material —not more, not less.

"Their voices do not last." Yet Caffarelli was famous for his youthful voice at the age of seventy; Orsini had triumphs in Prague when he was seventy-three, and when eighty-three he still sang for Maria Theresa of Austria, to help her relax and make her forget her heavy burdens. Matteucci's singing, "youthful and full of sweetness" until he died in his eighties, attracted people from far each time he sang to the praise of God in Naples' churches; last, not least, Bannieri—*l'enfant gâté* of Louis XIV (1643–1715)—who lived until he was one hundred and two years of age, still fascinated with his singing at the age of ninety-seven.

Whatever the reason for so much injustice may have been, the Italian *musici,* with their "disgusting" voices, evidently enchanted their listeners to a fantastic degree or they could never have been so beloved and idolized as to be immortalized on golden medals which adorned the necks of queens. They were overloaded with wealth and honors—"one God, one Farinelli" shouted London in 1733. "They are the image of heavenly music for which we know only the voices of Seraphs," are the words the scholar Grazioso Uberti uses when he refers to them in his book *Contrasto Musica.* Lod. Grignani, Rome, 1630.

La tua voce soave, allor che canti
Passa veloce dall' orecchio al core
Ivi desta il piacer, desta l'amore
E i piu tristi pensier fuggono erranti.
                    Domenico Cimarosa.[29]

[While you sing your sooth voice
Takes its road to the heart;
There delights, rouses love,
All low spirits depart.]
                    (Author's translation.)

. . . Et dans la voix, dans sa caresse
Reveillant le coeur endormi
Mêle aux soupirs de la maîtresse
L'accent plus mâle de l'ami.
                    Théophile Gautier.[30]

[. . . And in the voice, in its caress
That rouses the lethargic heart
Is mixed with sighing lady love
The virile wooer's robust part.]
                    (Author's translation.)

---

[29] Domenico Cimarosa (1749–1801) was orphaned when seven years of age. He received his fundamental vocal education from Father Polcano, the kind organist of the convent where little Domenico had found shelter. At the age of twelve he was admitted into the orphanage Madonna di Loreto, the famous conservatory which was discussed in this Part, footnote 23, p. 97. He remained there for eleven years, studying both voice and composition with Fedele Fenaroli (1730–1788) of the Scarlatti-Durante school, and later he became one of Aprile's best voice students. To understand fully the enormous influence of Naples' Scarlatti-Durante school, read the biographies of Scarlatti and Pergolesi (Part I, footnote 42, p. 29), of Aprile (the following page and its footnote 31), of Zingarelli (this Part, footnote 39, p. 108), of Vaccai (Part II, footnote 40, p. 73),

ALBERT, John: born in London, England, 1660–1724; contraltist, theorboist, composer. His song *The Pills to Purge Melancholy* (*Le pillole per purgare la malinconia*) was for many years a favorite throughout Europe. He was **the only English *musico* of fame.**

APRILE, Giuseppe: born in Martina, Apulia, 1732–1813; contraltist, composer, famous teacher; beautiful, pupil at Naples' conservatory Pietà dei Turchini of Girolamo Abos of the Scarlatti-Durante school, teacher of the just treated famous composer Cimarosa and of the Irish tenor Kelly, born O'Kelly and known in Italy as Occhelli.[31] Both Cimarosa and Kelly loved Aprile as long as they lived for his kindness. He sang throughout Europe, then taught in Naples. He wrote many *solfeggi* for his students; the best-known collection is *The Modern Italian Method of Singing*, London, 1791, published by Broderip.

BANNIERI, Antonio: born in Rome, 1638–1740; sopranist, *"l'enfant gâté"* of Louis XIV, knighted. He still sang at ninety-seven. Some biographies report him as French, but this is an error; the same sources report him also as educated by Louis XIV, forgetting that he was five years older than Louis XIV (1643–1715).

BERNACCHI, Antonio Maria, "the king of singers": born in Bologna, Emiglia, 1685–1756; sopranist, composer, graceful, vain, very kind, Handel singer, member of Bologna's Philharmonic Academy, pupil of Pistocchi for voice, one of the most famous singers and teachers we ever had, teacher of the court teacher Giambattista Mancini,[32] of the tenors Raaff (also Raff) and Carlani, of the

---

and of Battistini (Part I, footnote 7, p. 9). At S. M. Loreto Cimarosa also studied the violin, organ and harpsichord and became a distinguished violinist. Although he was early applauded in Italy, his rise to world-wide reputation came slowly. In 1789, he was called to the Russian court of Catherine II as a tenor, composer and voice teacher, and when he left, the Tsarina bade him farewell with a harpsichord that is still the pride of the Neapolitan conservatory. Subsequently, in 1792, while in the service of the Austrian court, he wrote *Il matrimonio secreto* at the order of Emperor Leopold II. The Emperor was so charmed by this jocose opera that he had it repeated the very same day of the first performance. **In this masterpiece Cimarosa reached the level of Mozart.** Of his thirty-one operas another masterpiece, *Le astuzie femminili,* was rearranged by Respighi (1879–1936) in 1920. Cimarosa was one of the first composers to use trios and quartets in opera.

[30] The Frenchman Théophile Gautier (1811–1872) was a poet and writer, a drama and music critic, a freethinker and witty aesthete. Sparkling jewels in the treasury of French literature are his novel *Mademoiselle de Maupin* and his collection of poems *Émaux et Camées*. The sense of beauty was so predominant in Gautier that he was completely indifferent to anything less than perfect beauty in art. He is the author of the aphorism: "Music is of all noises the most expensive and the most disagreeable one." How deeply he must have been moved to have written, ". . . And in the voice, in its caress . . ."

[31] It was for Kelly that Mozart wrote the part of Don Basilio in *Le Nozze di Figaro.*

[32] See Part II, footnote 26, p. 60.

primadonna Tesi, of the *musici* Amadori, Cusanino (see Cusanino), Guarducci, Gizziello (see Gizziello) . . . an endless chain of the best ones—and of Farinelli, the most famous of them all (see Farinelli).

Some biographies report that his voice was extremely poor in the beginning, so bad that both he and his friends doubted that he would ever make a career and that after he had become an adult the *musico* Pistocchi (see Pistocchi) who himself had gone through much vocal trouble helped him, but only after a long period of most painful restudying. Yet, Bernacchi had only one voice teacher— Pistocchi. He started to sing in Duesseldorf, Germany, when only sixteen years old, and he sang thereafter for more than thirty-five years, until 1736, when— still singing—he founded his famous school in Bologna. The truth is that since Bernacchi, immediately after his castration, was a rather weak and very narrow-chested youngster, Pistocchi, who loved this gifted and good-natured boy, had a difficult time until the head sounds of his favorite pupil were firmly anchored in his chest. Therefore Bernacchi later became a very great teacher, and therefore all his pupils were renowned for their powerful and insinuating high and low notes, for their clean and unique trills, and for their endless breath. Bernacchi had seen to it that their **perfectly trained head and falsetto voices were firmly anchored in their chests,** as Aristotle fought for in antiquity, as Tosi called for on page 14 (edition 1723) of his famous treatise *Opinioni* . . . (see Tosi), as Senesino more than half a century later emphasized in his *Instructions* . . . (see Senesino— F. Tenducci), as Vergine—again a century later (at the end of the nineteenth century) trained Caruso, and as is taught by all good teachers in every era— also today. May I suggest to all readers who are interested in vocal technique to now reread "The Registers and Their Union" in Part I of this manual.

Bernacchi was just as kind a human being as he was a great artist. Once (1727), in a rivalry between young Farinelli and himself, he did nothing but repeat impromptu all the acrobatics Farinelli had so well prepared and was singing to show off. He repeated from memory but nevertheless with longer breaths, with more finesse, and inserting his perfect trills of major and minor thirds (see p. 58). He won. The clever Farinelli then begged him to accept him as a pupil, and Bernacchi imparted to Farinelli all his art and wisdom.

CAFFARELLI (Gaetano Majorano): born in Bari, Apulia, 1703–1783; sopranist, composer, harpsichordist, beautiful, very conceited, died a duke, famous pupil of Porpora "the Patriarch of Harmony."[33] When seventy years old he was still famous for his youthful voice in perfect pitch.

He was the son of a very poor peasant, a day laborer. He spent the days of his childhood in Bari's churches, attracted by the music. He sang in the church choirs and continued singing the Masses in the streets. The composer Caffaro[34]

---

[33] See Part II, footnote 25, second para., p. 58.

[34] The composer Caffaro, the first patron of little Caffarelli, is not to be confused with the composer and court teacher Pasquale Cafaro (1706–1787) of the Scarlatti-Durante school.

observed the proud and beautiful child with the classic features, and recognized the unusual talent. He began to teach him to read, to write, and to understand the fundamentals of music; when he knew more about his little protégé, he suggested the operation. But the boy's father opposed all this with violence, and it took a long time to get his consent. Not until he was twelve years old was Gaetano Majorano sent to the "Pontifical Doctor." Afterwards he took the name Caffarelli in gratitude to his benefactor Caffaro, who sent him to study under the famous Porpora. In nearly all biographies of Caffarelli it is told in a legendary manner that Porpora made Caffarelli study for more than five years on one single sheet of music and told him after this period: "Go, my son, you are the greatest virtuoso of the world." This story loses its nebulous aspect right away when we consider that Porpora's one sheet of music contained not merely some exercises, as is generally believed, but that Porpora had sketched on it **all the basic exercises** he thought necessary for the training of Caffarelli's voice. While studying they were slowly developed in the length, forms, variations, and so forth required for training into artistry. Finally they were sung with some words. Thus, on one such sheet of basic exercises a student could very well learn every virtuosity, even to improvise. For a clear understanding of this kind of training see the fifth used as a basic exercise on *scalette* with its sample developments on pp. 40, 41. Porpora considered Caffarelli better than Farinelli. Handel, Porpora's rival, who always insisted upon having his compositions sung just as he had written them, let Caffarelli have his own way, so eager was he to have Caffarelli as interpreter for his operas. Moreover, Handel wrote many an opera part especially for Caffarelli's voice, for instance, the opening air in *Serse*.

Once, while singing in Naples, Caffarelli learned that sixteen year old but already famous Gizziello (see Gizziello) was making his Roman debut. Caffarelli rushed to Rome in a horse-drawn coach, traveling twenty-four hours. He ran to the theater at once, listened to Gizziello's first aria, and then shouted from his seat: "Bravo! Well done, Gizziello! It is Caffarelli who tells you this." Then he drove back to Naples, arriving just in time for his own operatic appearance. Somewhat later both he and Gizziello had to sing in Pergolesi's[35] *Adriano in Siria* at the inauguration of Naples' San Carlo theater. After Gizziello had heard Caffarelli sing his first aria, he had a breakdown: "I am lost; I shall never be able to equal him." Only because of the encouragement of Caffarelli did he dare to face San Carlo's crowded, critical pit. After that evening Gizziello was evaluated the best singer for sentiment, and Caffarelli the best and most brilliant virtuoso of vocal art. In 1755, in Lisbon, each was paid 72,000 gold francs for three months.

Caffarelli was also the highest paid singer in Italy. He was famous for his arrogance towards employers who wanted to humiliate him for his status. He loved to show off, and had a duel with the poet Ballot in Paris. There are many anecdotes dealing with his violence; one narrates how while in the service of Louis XV he killed with his hands his own starving father, reproaching the

---

[35] See Part I, footnote 42, second para., p. 29.

latter for his operation. Obviously this story originated in the brain of some enemy, because it was his father who had objected to the castration. Besides, Caffarelli was violent and haughty only towards those who wanted to humiliate him. If we consider the following episode we cannot blame him for such feelings. Once the Cardinal of Abbani wanted him to sing at a banquet he was giving. Caffarelli did not feel well; when the Cardinal sent for him, he was in his house robe and apologized for being unable to sing. Four strong men forced him thus clad into the car of the Cardinal, and he had to sing in this costume in front of the Cardinal's guests. After the concert he was beaten by order of the Cardinal for having "dared to appear in his house robe." The Cardinal's guests, who at first had cheered his singing, now cheered his being beaten up.

Caffarelli had many amorous adventures. Once, hiding from the rage of a jealous husband, he was forced to spend an entire night in an empty, damp well behind a sweetheart's home. As a result of this night a cold kept him in bed for more than a month, but not all his love affairs ended in a well.

He was immensely rich, and when he retired he decided to enter the ranks of the aristocracy. He bought an estate in Apulia to which the title of a papal duke was attached. Caffarelli, the son of a poor day laborer, now the "Duke of Santo Dorato," built two residences—a noble villa in the graceful Southern Baroque on his ducal estate, and a palace in the Vicolo delle Carminelle in the upper Toledo district of Naples. Over its entrance one could read the proud sentence *Amphyon*[36] *Thebas, ego domum* [Amphyon built Thebes, I this house]. Inside there was an enormous room with walls covered entirely with Venetian mirrors, charmingly engraved rococo jewels. Each morning the Duke of Santo Dorato entered this room followed by a servant dressed in the colors of the house who carried a golden tray with a wine bottle and a precious golden goblet. Old Caffarelli then lifted the goblet towards the mirrored walls and drank to the Duke's health, while the servant had to bow in reverence.

After his death his nephew and descendants became dukes of Santo Dorato. One of them removed all mirrors from Caffarelli's *sala ducale* [ducal chamber], but the palace was still standing before the Second World War.

CONFORTI (also Conforto), GIOVANNI LUCA: born in Mileto, Calabria, *ca.* 1560–16??; contraltist, composer, church singer, pupil of Claudio Merulo,[37] teacher.

As previously reported in the Survey, Conforti was the first "Italian" contraltist in the papal service (from 1580 to 1585, and again in 1591). He also was the first "Italian" *castrato* to publish his teachings, *Breue et facile maniera...*, which include the *Dichiaratione sopra li passaggi*, Rome, 1593 and not—as often stated—

---

[36] Amphyon in Greek mythology was a son of Zeus who became a great singer and musician. He erected seven-gated Thebes in Boeotia.

[37] The composer Claudio Merulo (1533–1604) belonged to the best precursors of the Venetian school that became, through Giovanni Gabrieli (1557–1612), the cradle of Bel Canto. See Part II, Chapter I: A: §1. Explanation of the Expression "Bel Canto," p. 37.

1583 or 1603. This small textbook is most interesting because it reveals the struggle in those remote days of growing musicianship for musical embellishments which later matured into the unique virtuosities of Bel Canto. The year before, in 1592, Conforti had reintroduced into music the medieval *pressus* that had been forbidden by Pope John XXII. He named it *trillo* [trill] and used this new term in 1593 on page 25 of the just mentioned *Breue et . . .* A short outline of the trill's history may be found in Part II, Chapter I: A: §2. V. of this manual.

CRESCENTINI, GIROLAMO, the "Italian Orpheus": born in a hamlet near Urbino in the Pontifical States, the Marches, 1766–1846; sopranist, composer, excellent actor, knighted, pupil of Lorenzo Gibelli, Bologna.[38]

Crescentini was one of the last eminent virtuosi, he had one of the sweetest voices ever known, and he sang throughout all Europe.

When Napoleon I was in Vienna in 1805 on his march to conquer the world, he heard him sing the part of Romeo in Zingarelli's opera *Romeo e Giulietta*. In the third act he always sang his own famous insertion *Ombra adorata aspetta* [Adored shadow, wait]. When Napoleon heard him sing it, he could not control his emotions; he wept like a child, as did his entire staff. After the performance Napoleon on the spot knighted him with the Iron Crown. But this was not all. Napoleon, usually not too sentimental, could not forget Crescentini's voice. He longed to hear him again; he called him to his court, and wherever he drove during the succeeding years, Crescentini had to follow him, and had to sing whenever Napoleon felt depressed from the strain of his restless life. There was nothing Napoleon would have denied him. Thus, when Napoleon in 1806 reorganized Italy after it had been completely conquered and freed, he kept his promise. He **outlawed boy castration throughout all Italy.** When, on February 2, 1808, Rome was occupied by the French army, it was outlawed there too, and as long as the Pontifical States were under French occupation this law had to be most strictly obeyed. Even when, after the fall of Napoleon, Francis I of Austria (1768–1835) became again the hated sovereign of the greater part of Northern Italy, this law not only remained effective for this region, but was reinforced, because now, besides the outlawing of the operation, no *musico* was allowed to appear in a woman's role in the Kingdom of Lombardy-Venetia.

Only in Rome castration was revived immediately after the reinstalment of the pope's sovereignty. But it had become outmoded. The young composers no longer wrote for the voices of the *musici*.

It is wrong to belittle artists like Crescentini, Farinelli, Ferri, Tosi and so forth, who instead of abusing their court influence used it for the benefit of their fellow-

---

[38] Gibelli, 1719–1812, had been—like F. G. Bertoni, the teacher of Pacchierotti—one of the many pupils of voice and composition of Bologna's famous Father Martini (see Part II, footnote 16, p. 43). The latter called Gibelli *"Il mio primo sopranetto"* [my chief little soprano]. Gibelli also belonged to the teachers of the Liceo Filarmonico—later called the Liceo Musicale—in Bologna who taught Rossini.

men in times when the average man was without rights. But it is just as wrong to wish the revival of this institution, because in all their glory, in all their triumphs, they felt extremely unhappy and miserable.

Crescentini remained in Paris until 1812, when he asked Napoleon to allow him to go home, since he suffered greatly from the Parisian climate. He left in May, before Napoleon's declaration of war upon Russia, on June 22, 1812.

Zingarelli wrote for Crescentini *Romeo e Giulietta,* the already mentioned opera that brought both Zingarelli and Crescentini very close to Napoleon's heart; Cimarosa wrote for Crescentini *Gli Orazi e Curiazi,* Rossini in 1823 *Seminamide,* and many other composers also wrote especially for his voice.[39]

CUSANINO (GIOVANNI CARESTINI): born in a village near Ancona, the Marches, *ca.* 1705–1760; contraltist of enormous range, excellent actor, handsome, a pupil of Bernacchi (see Bernacchi).

Giovanni Carestini took the name Cusanino out of gratitude to the wealthy family Cusano of Milan, who had paid for his operation and his subsequent excellent education. They had provided very generously for handsome Giovanni,

---

[39] Nicola Zingarelli (1752–1837) was born in Naples. Twenty years after his death his native city erected a monument in his honor in Saint Dominic Major, one of the oldest churches in Naples, dating from 1255, where he had been buried. When only seven years of age, Zingarelli received a scholarship to the conservatory of Madonna di Loreto. There he studied for ten years, first the violin, the harpsichord, Italian and Latin literature, and later, conducting and counterpoint as well, under the guidance of the famous Fedele Fenaroli. After having left San Loreto he continued his studies of counterpoint with the priest Speranza, who, like his previous teacher, Fenaroli, was one of Durante's master pupils. Zingarelli was extremely poor, and having no patron when he had to leave San Loreto, he started his career bravely as a private violin teacher in Torre Annunziata, a little town in the environs of Naples. He suffered greatly in those days, but his perseverance bore full fruits, because the self-respecting Zingarelli became a very successful composer. He wrote twenty-eight operas, the best of which is *Romeo e Giulietta* (1796), many songs, some ingenious *solfeggi,* pure instrumental music, and a huge phalanx of excellent ecclesiastical compositions, of which the *Miserere* of the year 1826 is a deeply touching gem. It is written for four voices and was first sung in 1827, during Lent, by two hundred students of the Royal College of Music, which, by then, had moved from its first seat, San Sebastiano, to the monastery of San Pietro a Maiella, where the conservatory of Naples still is located. The Royal College of Music of Saint Sebastian (Reale Collegio di Musica di San Sebastiano) had been founded in 1806 as the substitute for the four conservatories of Naples (see this Part, footnote 23, first para., p. 97). In 1813, Murat, Napoleon Bonaparte's brother-in-law and "King of Naples" since 1808, nominated, on Napoleon's orders, Zingarelli *Director of the Royal College of Music.* Zingarelli, the *first* director of this new school, was the *last* outstanding teacher of Naples' famous Scarlatti-Durante school (see this Part, footnote 29, p. 102). Among his many pupils were Saverio Mercadante, Carlo Conti, Morlacchi, Petrella and the genius Bellini.

For Cimarosa, see this Part, footnote 29, p. 102.

wanting their little *protégé* to miss nothing. He started his opera career when only sixteen years of age, sang throughout Europe, and belonged to the famous Handel singers. In this capacity he was Farinelli's opponent in London's rivalries between Porpora and Handel. Cusanino had a most powerful voice, and, never satisfied with himself, did not stop studying—maybe because he, the Adonis, the big mime, had lost in the struggle for supremacy against the very ugly Farinelli, who was no mime at all. Cusanino was the most modest and serious of the star *musici,* and harbored no resentment against Farinelli.

FARINELLI (Carlo Broschi) "of the divine trill": born in Naples, 1705–1782; sopranist, composer, poet, harpsichordist, viola d'amore player, very ugly, extremely clever, member of Bologna's Philharmonic Academy, statesman, knighted, first a pupil of Porpora,[40] later a pupil of Bernacchi (see Bernacchi).

Carlo Broschi was the son of a miller, whence, according to some historians, his name Farinelli derived, *farina* meaning "flour." Others believe that he—like many castrated boys of those days—named himself after his benefactors, the three brothers Farina, who had paid for the operation, had maintained him, and had paid for all his studies. He made his opera debut at the early age of fifteen in Naples, 1720, where he was called "the child."

Nearly all biographies of Farinelli report that this debut occured in the opera *Angelica e Medoro,* that the libretto was by the later famous young poet Pietro Metastasio (1698–1782), that this was Metastasio's first libretto, and that from then on the two artists were united in deepest friendship which lasted throughout all their lives. They called themselves and were called "the Twins." Yet such reports are erroneous, because Porpora's *Angelica e Medoro* was only performed in 1722, while Farinelli had made his debut in opera two years earlier. Neither was this Metastasio's first performed libretto. Many had been applauded before. The first one was *Il Giustino* in 1712, when this genius was a boy of only fourteen years (Florimo, *La scuola musicale di Napoli,* 1882).

The famous friendship between "the Twins" developed and matured throughout the years, while the castrated child Farinelli and the adult poet Metastasio both eagerly studied music with Porpora.

Farinelli was a brave boy. In 1722, when merely seventeen and after only two years of operatic experience, he sang once in Rome in his teacher's (Porpora) opera *Eumeme.* He had to trill on a high note with the clarinet player, a virtuoso in his art, who wanted personal applause. The latter held the note longer than they had rehearsed it—until he could do so no longer; but young Farinelli, well aware of the trap, used all his skill. When the clarinet player had to stop, he continued on the very same breath, on and on, and while the audience sat spellbound waiting for the end, he added—still on the same breath— an extempore cadence full of agilities. This was his first great triumph. If we

---

[40] See Part II, footnote 25, second para., p. 58.

consider that he was later outdone by Bernacchi, we can imagine what astounding breath power the star *musici* possessed.

Farinelli was a very clever man. His mind grasped quickly, and he never rejected advice or felt hurt if any was given to him, even after he had become a court favorite. Once, Charles VI of Austria, who was an excellent musician (see Orsini), said in Vienna to Farinelli (1731): "You are a good artist; why not become a great one? Your singing does not touch the heart. Yet it would be easy for you if in your creations you would be more simple and sincere. Think about it, it is worth while." Farinelli took this advice and some years later, when called upon to sing by his old teacher Porpora, then the embittered rival of Handel in the fight for supremacy in London, London shouted "one God, one Farinelli." Yet his opponent there was—as previously reported—Cusanino, born in the same year as Farinelli, a pupil of Bernacchi, as was Farinelli, and a famous virtuoso, as was Farinelli. Besides, the handsome and majestic Cusanino was an excellent actor, while the very ugly and oversized Farinelli was handicapped in his acting by spiderlike limbs. He never played with his hands, never moved his arms, and stood firm whenever it was possible, because one day, while he was still studying his first operatic roles, his brother Richard[41] had told him: "If you move your arms, your audience will giggle and titter; if you have none, they will listen and rave."

Only once in his life was Farinelli so excited that he forgot the oversize of his limbs; only once, and then it made a sad king giggle, a very melancholic king who, only minutes before, had been deeply stirred by Farinelli's singing. This happened in June, 1737, when Farinelli came to Spain, with the intention of singing in London in the fall. Arriving at the court of Philip V of Spain, he was ordered to appear before the Queen. The King suffered from misanthrophy; gloomily he refused to govern his country, to attend the council, to receive his ministers; he even refused to change his clothes and to shave. The worried Queen received Farinelli; she explained the entire situation, and asked him to sing in the room next to the one in which the brooding King idly passed his days. When King Philip heard Farinelli's jubilant runs, when he heard this gorgeous singing full of heavenly joy, he could not resist. Enchanted, he asked to

---

[41] Richard Broschi, 1701–1756 was the brother of Farinelli. When Richard was only a little boy of nine years he was the first music teacher of five years old Carlo, later Farinelli. Richard studied at Naples' Conservatory Maria di Loreto with the famous Durante while Carlo studied at the Onofrio with Porpora. **This shows again how the poorest boys in Italy, if really gifted, had access to the teaching of the greatest men of their time.** Richard became a composer and his compositions were promoted by Farinelli. Both Broschi became members of Bologna's Philharmonic Academy. Richard was also for a while a teacher and composer at the court of Duke Alexander of Württemberg, one of the German courts where throughout hundreds of years boys with no voices or bad ones were uselessly castrated (see this Part, footnote 23, second para., p. 97). Richard Broschi ended his career in Spain as Minister of War and of the Imperial Marine, an appointment that reveals in Farinelli a "little Napoleon."

see the singing god. When Farinelli entered, he said: "You have uplifted my heart, speak, and every wish of yours I will fulfill." Farinelli knew he had to bring the King back to an active life; knew that he had been called to the Spanish court only for this reason. Such a mission had never been assigned to him before. In his excitement he forgot the oversize of his limbs; kneeling down in front of the King he opened wide his long, long arms and shouted in his high-pitched voice: "Majesty, I pray you, call your barber and have him shave you." The King could not help it, he had to giggle. Smiling, he called for his barber, and two hours later a clean and shaved king asked Farinelli again what he wanted as a reward for his felicitous singing. Farinelli, having by now been well instructed by the ministers, asked the King to attend again his council, to govern his lands, and to sign the accumulated decrees. The King agreed, but said: "If I have to endure all these rascals, you too will have to endure them." He started a new life, but never allowed Farinelli to leave his side. Every evening, as long as King Philip lived, Farinelli had to sing for him the very same aria which had enchanted the ailing King the first time he heard it.

Farinelli became the shadow of Philip V. The courtiers who at first had ignored him, soon had to recognize in him the incorruptible man who guided Spain's destinies. He had no rank, but he was the real head of Spain's government for nearly twenty-two years. During all those years the misanthropic King, as well as his successor, signed no declaration of war. There is many an anecdote about these days, not a single one in disfavor of this gigantic eunuch, who in the eighteenth century proved again what many centuries earlier the Persian kings had known so well—that there is no man more trustworthy than a trusted eunuch.

Farinelli's salary was the highest that any man at the Spanish court ever received. He had not only his own servants and torchbearers but an entire personal escort, a golden state equipage, and he had a nobleman as his personal adjutant to take his orders.

After the death of Philip V (1746) he remained with the new king, Ferdinand VI, who was a modest and retiring man and who was still more under Farinelli's influence than his father had been. He even secured an old Neapolitan aristocratic lineage of highest degree for Carlo Broschi, born in a lowly mill of Naples' *bassifondi* [slums], so that he could nominate him *Chancellor of Calatrava*, which was Spain's highest distinction and could be given only to a man of noble birth. Under Ferdinand VI, Farinelli became the absolute ruler of Spain. He regulated the Tagus, ordered ships for the amusement of the court in Aranjuez. Dreaming of Venice, the artist Farinelli organized in Aranjuez serenades with flower battles and artistic contests. From 1747–1758 the Spanish opera, of which he was the director, gave fantastic performances there. He himself sang, and he called such stars as the *musici* Guarducci, Gizziello, Amadori, the tenors Garlani and Raaff, and the primadonnas Tesi and Mingotti. Never had the aristocracy of Spain heard or seen such fairylike summer nights.

With Ferdinand's death (1759) life changed abruptly for Farinelli. The new king, Charles III (1716–1788), a half brother of Ferdinand who disliked music and considered opera a "dangerous vice," dismissed Farinelli the very day he assumed the government of his country. He was a righteous man, and he continued to pay Farinelli the promised life stipend, but he sent him his passport—the polite invitation to leave the country in ten days.

Farinelli went home to Italy, but he could not settle for good in Naples, because it stood under Spanish mastery. From the profits of his English earnings he built a sumptuous villa in the midst of a huge orchard at the outskirts of Bologna. He baptized his new home *Follia Inglese* [English Folly] and filled it with all his many Spanish treasures. He took his sister and three of her children into his home and passed the following twenty-three years between the church, where he knelt for hours in deep devotion, and his villa—singing, playing on one of his many precious harpsichords (it is narrated that he possessed more than twelve of them), or playing the *viola d'amore*[42]—a Bergonzi and King Philip's first gift. It had been made especially for Farinelli and carried the King's dedication burned into the inner side of its body. He also composed in his *ritiro* [retreat] under his Murillos and Riberas. All doors to society were open to him; he developed a close friendship with Father Martini; he helped financially the studying young *musici* of Bologna, although he never took any particular interest in any of them, never asked any of them to sing, or helped with his knowledge. Many a statesman, scholar, and sovereign came from faraway to Bologna with the sole aim of visiting Farinelli and hearing him sing, for his voice never lost its enchantment. But the very rich Farinelli, always "bewigged and full-dressed" in most precious garments, as if just going to court, was a brokenhearted, sad old man who went three times daily to church to pray for ... Spain. He never used any of his high titles; he even avoided the name Farinelli, modestly calling himself now Carlo Broschi. He sickened after the death of his "Twin," and died five months after the latter.

There are two very ugly spots in Farinelli's life, which are seldom reported. They show us a different Farinelli from the man pictured mostly as having been unselfish and kind. When his best friend, Metastasio, wrote that old Porpora was in utmost need and sick in Naples, Farinelli disregarded the call for help; and when Metastasio again and again begged for this old man who had always given much more than he had received, Farinelli tightly closed his purse.—During the years he spent in Follia Inglese, Matteo, his nephew and heir who lived with him, married. Farinelli fell in love with Matteo's young wife. Under some pretext he sent the nephew on a trip. When the young woman refused his advances, he locked her up in the upper story of the mansion, made life miserable for her, and made an old jealous fool out of himself.

---

[42] The shape and construction of the *viola d'amore* resembled those of our viola; the size was larger. It had seven gut strings in conformity with the seven notes of the scale which were stopped on a fingerboard. Besides, it had seven or more wire strings passing beneath the board and vibrating with the gut strings; it was played with a bow.

FERRI, Baldassare: born in Perugia, Umbria, 1610–1680; sopranist, a singer of the standing of Farinelli, tall, handsome, with perfect manners, magnanimous, twice knighted.

Ferri started his career at the early age of eleven. He was the first star *musico* to be called from court to court and to become immensely rich. He could sing on one single breath a chromatic scale of trills of two octaves up and down again on a *messa di voce* of about fourteen measures in *tempo moderato,* while clearly marking each single step and ending the trilled scale with a complicated closure.

Queen Christina of Sweden sent a ship of her luxurious, private flotilla for him, in which nothing was missing for his comfort. She heaped honors and gifts on him. She had a medal struck, showing on one side the singer's head wreathed with laurels, and on the reverse a swan dying on the banks of the Meander river, while a lyre descended from Heaven.

One evening after he had sung in London, a masked figure suddenly grabbed his hand, slipped on his finger a ring with an emerald of enormous value, and disappeared. He never knew from whom it had come.

For twenty years he was in service at the court in Vienna (1655–1675). Leopold I of Austria (born in 1640, emperor from 1658 to 1705), whose Majesty—the story goes—Ferri had often sung into slumber, had a painting made of him. It carried the inscription: baldassare ferri perugino, musicorum rex [king of the *musici*], and the young emperor had this portrait hung in his bedroom. He also knighted Ferri and gave him a big life stipend.

In Venice there was no end to the honors that were heaped on him, and there again he was knighted. Yet Ferri remained simple and modest, with his money bag open to everyone in need. Nobody had to come begging; he willingly gave to all musicians, and especially to all *musici*. He also left his immense fortune to the poor.

GIZZIELLO (Giovacchino Conti): born in Arpino,[43] Southern Latium, 1714–1761; sopranist, beautiful, of very fine character, disciple of the very famous voice teacher, composer and tenor Domenico Gizzi (also known as Egizio) of the Neapolitan school.

Giovacchino Conti was seven years old when he was castrated, but could not gain admission into any of Naples' overcrowded conservatories. Gizzi, who had opened a private voice school in Naples in 1720, heard of the misfortune of his young fellow citizen. Gizzi, too, was an Arpinate. He took the child into his home with the intention of sheltering him for some months. He kept him seven years, asked no money, raised him, taught him, and made an artist of him, because he had grown extremely fond of the charming child. As a sign of gratitude Conti took the name Gizziello.

---

[43] Arpino, the Roman Arpinum, a town in the province of Frosinone, Latium, was the cradle of many famous men. Two of her greatest sons are the Romans Marius (158 b.c.–87 b.c.) and Cicero (106 b.c.–43 b.c.).

He made his debut on February 4th, 1730 in Rome at the early age of sixteen years in Leonardo Vinci's[44] opera *Artaserse* (see Pacchierotti), and when seventeen he sang with Caffarelli (see Caffarelli) in Naples. He was one of the youngest Handel singers and one of the best. Nevertheless, after these successes, he studied for some time with Bernacchi (see Bernacchi). Then, as previously reported, he sang in Lisbon with Caffarelli, where he was paid 72.000 gold francs for three months, and at the Spanish court under Farinelli, as well as with him (see Farinelli). He was cherished by Europe's audiences for his faultless art, and adored by his fellow singers for the charm of his character.

GUADAGNI, GAETANO: born in Lodi, Lombardy, 1725–1792 (Brunelli, *I Teatri di Padova,* 1921); contraltist, composer, excellent actor, beautiful, knighted.

He sang Handel's *Messiah* and *Samson* in perfect English; when twenty-seven years old he created Gluck's *Il Telemacco* and *Orfeo,* and the result was a deep friendship between him and Gluck (1714–1787). Never satisfied with his accomplishments, he went to Lisbon with the intention of studying with his idol Gizziello, although he himself was already famous. He studied with the latter daily for more than one year and became one of the top star sopranists (Charles Burney). The beautiful and haughty Guadagni was always having love affairs with the prettiest ladies of the European aristocracy, but he was too clever ever to get into real trouble. Venice bestowed on him the knighthood of San Marco.

MARCHESI, LUIGI (also Marchesini): born in Milan, 1754–1829; sopranist, composer whose songs were published in Vienna and London, beautiful, good actor, very generous, vainglorious, knighted, pupil of the *musico* Caironi and the tenor Albuzzi.

He was an outstanding virtuoso whose repertory comprehended nearly all operas of his time. He could trill from the lowest to the highest note of his range in a faultless scale and down again on one single breath. He sang throughout all Europe and was for years at the opera of Saint Petersburg. When he came home from his European glories, the Academy of Milan had a golden medal struck in his honor. Soon Venice, Siena, Florence, and Trieste also carved his head to be put on medals, which were worn around the necks of the belles. Marchesi showed himself very magnanimous when Milan's conservatory was founded, and he was always generous when a fellow artist needed help.

Yet he was not merely a magnanimous and superb artist but also vain in a most eccentric way. When the curtain rose in a theater where he happened to be the star performer, he would stand on a rock (the *Marchesirock!*) draped in

---

[44] The composer Leonardo Vinci (1690–1730) of the famous Neapolitan school is not to be confused with the universal genius Leonardo da Vinci (1452–1519). *Artaserse* was the last and best of Leonardo Vinci's many operas and its libretto was written by Pietro Metastasio, Farinelli's previously mentioned "Twin." The aria *Vo' solcando un mar crudele,* G. Ricordi, would be worthy of being revived.

red brocade, wearing a helmet with many-colored feathers upon his wig, girt with a sword, brandishing a shining lance in his right hand, and holding a huge jeweled shield in his left. In answer to the call of a horn he would sing from the rock his first lines, always the same ones, stating that "his ears had heard his beloved audience's call." Then he would descend from his rocky eminence in a most majestic manner and sing his *aria di baule*[45] [suitcase song], a love song that stated how an unhappy love had damaged his tender heart. Only after such a pompous introduction was the opera performance permitted to start. Once, as he was descending majestically from the rock, he stumbled and fell. Impeded by all the paraphernalia he was wearing, he could not get back on his feet. He lay flat on his stomach, the helmet covered his eyes . . . and now the real artist rose above the spoiled fool. He improvised in this situation an entire aria: *Misericordia, perdono* . . . [*Mercy, forgiveness* . . .]. The audience raved, and the defeat—so well prepared by some jealous enemy—turned into his greatest triumph.

MATTEUCCI, Matteo (Marquis Matteo Sassani), *L'usignolo di bella Napoli* [the nightingale of beautiful Naples]: born in Naples, 1649-after 1730; very famous sopranist, a delicate beauty. He is not to be confounded with Pietro Mattuci, who also was a famous sopranist (*ca.* 1768–*ca.* 1830). Matteucci's caressing voice still enchanted when he sang in Naples' churches at the age of eighty. **He was the only *musico* who was of noble birth.**

MELANI FAMILY—a Tuscan Tale from the Arabian Nights.

Long ago, at the beginning of the seventeenth century, Domenico Melani was the ever-gaily-singing litter carrier of the Bishop of Pistoia. Melani had eight children; all were boys, and it was the ambitious dream in Melani's hut that they should become good musicians. The bishop liked his singing litter carrier and helped him. To all eight boys he granted such a good education that each of them turned out a fine artist. Alessandro, Antonio, and Jacopo became composers and choir masters; the other five—Atto, Bartolomeo, Domenico, Filippo, and Nicola were sent one after the other to be evirated, and then were bountifully provided for and carefully trained, so that all five became very acceptable and well paid court singers. Bartolomeo and Filippo, the monk, also distinguished themselves in opera. The education of the *musico* Atto (1626–1714), a priest, had been so very refined that, over and above being applauded in opera as a sopranist and estimated as a composer, he became in his later years the artful Tuscan ambassador to mighty France. Alessandro Caccia, the kind bishop, did

---

[45] The *aria di baule* was a song composed by, or especially for a singer of those days to display the artist at his best. He always carried it along, hence the name "suitcase song." Some singers inserted the very same *aria di baule* into every opera, even if out of place. It had been introduced by Senesino (Francesco Bernardi). For the latter's biography see this Part, The *Musici*, p. 120. The last niche for a "suitcase song," and still in use, is "the lesson" in Rossini's *The Barber of Seville*.

not stop there. He found a musical niche even for old Domenico, and father Melani died as the proudest bellringer of Pistoia's cathedral.

MORESCHI, ALESSANDRO (*Monsignore*[46]): born in Monte Comparti, a small town near Rome, 1858–1922; sopranist, conductor, educated in the Schola Cantorum di S. Salvatore in Lauro in Rome, later pupil of Gaetano Capocci; **the last musico.**

Moreschi, surnamed *l'angelo di Roma* [the angel of Rome], was admitted to the newly founded pontifical school for boy singers, the Schola Cantorum di S. Salvatore in Lauro[47] in Rome, when thirteen years of age. He stayed all his life in the service of the Pontifical Church and, after Mustafà, was then its best soloist. He belonged to the Sistine Chapel (1883–1913), to the Lateran Chapel of Saint John (Cappella Lateranense di S. Giovanni), and later also to the Julian Chapel of St. Peter's (Cappella Giulia di S. Pietro in Vaticano). In addition, he sang for the aristocracy and for Rome's famous *circoli*, exclusive regional clubs, which were highly influential centers of art . . . and also of politics, and which were abolished by Mussolini under the pretext that they were maiming Italy by a partisan approach to national questions. Wherever timid *Monsignore* Moreschi sang, the frenzy of joy took hold of the listening crowds, not only in Italy but also in France.

He was the only *musico* whose voice has been recorded. Recordings of those days—as we all know—were unable to do justice to a soprano's notes above a^2

, if the voice was blessed with high frequencies, as was the superb soprano of Angelica Pandolfini, for example. Much less could they reproduce all the overtones in the voice of a *musico*.

I heard "the angel of Rome" for the last time in 1912 and never again felt a similar delight, not in Caruso's *La donna è mobile,* not in the trance Casals' cello still produces.[48] Considering that Moreschi as well as Mustafà were very far beneath the level of a Farinelli or Ferri, vocally as well as artistically, it is understandable that so often mighty and spoiled sovereigns bowed in enchantment before some poor *musico* who sang as no living person has heard singing.

MUSTAFÀ, DOMENICO: born in a hamlet near Foligno, Umbria, 1829–1912; sopranist, composer, conductor, knighted, pupil of Tobilli of the Sistine Chapel, and pupil of Addrizza; **the last star musico.**

---

[46] See this Part, footnote 14, p. 95.

[47] See this Part, Survey, p. 94.

[48] The Spanish cellist, composer and conductor, the noble fighter for freedom Pablo Casals "who turns a concert hall into a temple," born in 1876 and still unsurpassed as cellist . . . unsurpassed, too, in his love for freedom.

He was a boy of only thirteen when his first Mass was successfully preformed, and at that time he was already a vocal virtuoso. At nineteen he entered the Sistine Chapel as a sopranist, in 1874 the Pope made him "Permanent Director of the Pontifical Chapel." One of his greatest triumphs was the revival of Palestrina in Paris in 1892, when Paris went frantic over Mustafà the vocal virtuoso and Mustafà the sublime conductor. His masterpiece, *Tu es Petrus,* is to be heard in St. Peter's greatest ceremonies. Beautiful, too, are his motet *O salutaris ostia* and his *Dies Irae* for seven voices.

ORSINI, GAETANO: born in Rome (?), 1667–1750; contraltist, knighted.

He entered the service of the Austrian court at the age of twenty-one and remained there until he died. He sang for the extremely sensitive Leopold I (1658–1705) (see Ferri), for Joseph I (1705–1711), and for Charles VI (1711–1740), who, all three, were very good instrumentalists, and composers too. Finally, he sang for his revered pupil, the Empress Maria Theresa (1740–1780). From childhood, the Empress had carried all her sorrows and worries—all her secrets to this great and sincere artist, who had never tired of singing the most artistic fantasias for her lullabies, and who had always been her very best friend. Orsini's life, like that of Farinelli, proves again that there is no man more trustworthy than a trusted eunuch.

PACCHIEROTTI, GASPARE (also Pacchiarotti), "master of every style": born in Fabriano, the Marches, 1744–1821; famous sopranist, excellent musician who sang the most difficult parts without rehearsing, very ugly and thin, introvert, magnanimous, pupil of Ferdinando Giuseppe Bertoni, Venice,[49] famous teacher.

He belonged first to the singers of the Chapel of Saint Mark's in Venice and did not make his opera debut until he was twenty-two years of age. He was a high sopranist whose notes above c^3 (the female high c) remained sweet, flexible, and as full as is the g^2 (the g above the fifth line) of an excellent dramatic soprano of our day. He was famous—and often envied—for his flood of trilled melodies, which he could produce as though they came from a lark high in the sky.

No two reports concerning his life correspond. Monaldi and many other historians praise him for never having sung the same cadences and for having been an improviser on the level of Farinelli, while de Martini[50] in his *Histoire du chant* blames him for never in his entire career having changed his repertory, and having therefore been monotonous and boring. But the same de Martini narrates, in conformity with most others, that when Pacchierotti sang with the *primadonna*

[49] Bertoni, 1725–1813, had been—like Gibelli, the teacher of Crescentini—one of the many pupils of Bologna's famous Father Martini. For Father Martini see Part II, footnote 16, p. 43; for Gibelli see this Part, footnote 38, p. 107.

[50] Aug. de Martini of the Paris conservatory is not to be confused with Bologna's Father Martini.

Gabrielli,[51] the latter was so moved by his caressing voice that she could not keep back her tears, while Monaldi says that Gabrielli and her mighty lover Ruffo, jealous of Pacchierotti's artistic superiority, wanted to destroy him and that they persecuted him most violently until they had reached their aim so thoroughly that Pacchierotti never sang again. Monaldi even tells that Caffarelli assisted Ruffo in his fight against Pacchierotti, which attitude would by no means fit into the character of the very proud Caffarelli, who hated all oppressors and surely never would have helped one in power to use it against some *musico* (see Caffarelli).

Another story tells how once, in Rome, while rehearsing the part of Arbace in Leonardo Vinci's opera *Artaserse*, Pacchierotti noticed that the orchestra had stopped playing while he sang *E pur sono innocente* [And yet I am innocent]. When he asked for the reason, the conductor who sat at the harpsichord answered: "We cannot play, we are weeping." However, this anecdote is also narrated with the very same background and details of Gizziello, who made his debut in the opening performance of this opera on February 4, 1730 (see Gizziello), fourteen years before Pacchierotti was born and thirty-six years before the latter was ready for his opera debut. It one considers that a composer of those days of creative over-production seldom remained in vogue over so long a period, it seems highly doubtful that Pacchierotti ever sang Vinci's *Artaserse*. But such contrasting and confusing reports show how cherished, how greatly admired this artist had been. There is a painting from the year 1710 with Tosi (see Tosi) at the harpsichord; copies of it can be found in biographies of Pacchierotti, attributing it to Pacchierotti, who was born in 1744.

Pacchierotti, universally appreciated as a teacher, left enclosed in his will counsels for voice students, in the form of fifteen commandments. They can be found in the unique library of Bologna's Liceo Musicale, and are full of wisdom.

PISTOCCHI, Francesco Antonio: born in Palermo, Sicily, 1659–1726; contraltist, composer, one of the greatest teachers, **founder of the famous Bolognese school,** priest, monk, extremely kind, member of Bologna's Philharmonic Academy, pupil of his father, teacher of the tenor Fabri, of the *musici* Bernacchi "the king of singers" (see Bernacchi), Minelli (who like his teacher became a priest), Pasi, Riccieri (see Riccieri), Bartolini,[52] and very many others.

---

[51] Caterina Gabrielli, *La Romanina* [the little one of Rome], 1730–1796, was the daughter of a cook in the household of the Roman Prince Gabrielli. The prince who was her godfather paid for her very good general education and also for her vocal education with Porpora (see Part II, footnote 25, second para., p. 58). Gabrielli was far the best of the few female artists who existed while the art of the *musici* reached its zenith. She was applauded throughout all Europe; she had everywhere amatory affairs with the mightiest men of her time—with a preference for royal blood. Besides, she was the sweetheart of the thirty-two years older Pietro Metastasio (see Farinelli), whom she adored.

[52] Pistocchi's star pupil and court singer Bartolomeo Bartolini, born in Faenza, *ca.* 1685–17??, is not to be confused with the first Italian sopranist, Simone Bartolini (Simon

Francesco Antonio, born in Palermo of parents from Cesena, always claimed to be a Bolognese, exactly as did Tosi of Cesena, his contemporary. Although it sounds incredible, it is narrated that he sang at the age of three years in a concert where he was taken seriously and much applauded; when he was five years old his singing enchanted the Grand Duke of Tuscany and the cardinals who had called for him to sing in Bologna's Sette Chiese [Seven Churches]; when he was eight years old he composed *Capricci puerili saviamente composti* . . . Bologna, G. Monti, 1667, which may be found in the library of Bologna's Liceo Musicale. These *capricci* of an eight year old boy are full of creative fancy and written for harpsichord, harp, violins, violoncellos, and so forth.

This genius, whose parents were so poor that they made use of their little boy to earn some money, and who never had enough to eat, was too frail for his beautiful soprano voice to mature after castration. When at the age of twenty "Pistocchino" [tiny Pistocchi] finally made his opera debut as a sopranist, the voice proved too weak.

Unhappy and frustrated, he became a priest, and many years later, in 1715, when already a famous voice teacher, he became a monk. However, neither the priest nor the monk ever stopped composing, singing, or teaching. Ten years after his first tragic opera appearance, at the age of thirty, the priest Pistocchi again tried to face an audience. He sang as contraltist and was applauded, but this more for the deep culture of his singing than for the richness and amplitude of his vocal organs. From that time on he sang continuously and was a well-liked singed and composer. Moreover, he started a voice school which brought him enormous fame.

He was one of the finest and one of the unhappiest *musici*. He died very poor and much beloved, for he had brought joy and help to all who had crossed his road; in memory of him many Italian cities have a *via* or *viale Pistocchi*. A spark of this tender soul, worth being revived, dances in his French song *Je me fais un plaisir,* G. Ricordi.

PORPORINO, UBERTI (Anton Hubert): born in Verona, Venetia, 1697–1783; contraltist, full of charm and grace, knighted.

The German boy Anton Hubert took the name Porporino out of respect and gratitude to his teacher Porpora,[53] who had been very kind to him. He entered the service of Frederic the Great at the latter's court in Berlin. He remained there as a court singer for forty-two years, singing until his death at the age of eighty-six—the typical life of a star *musico*.

PRATO, VINCENZO DEL: born at Imola, Emilia, 1756–1828; sopranist. Mozart

---

Perusinus), who is treated in this Part, Survey, p. 96 and its footnote 17, nor to be confused with Vincenzo Bartolini, another sopranist in the endless scores of court singers in the eighteenth century.

[53] See Part II, footnote 25, second para., p. 58.

(1756–1791) wrote for his voice the part of Idamante in the opera *Idomeneo,* which had its first performance in 1781 at the court theater of Munich.

RICCIERI (also Ricieri), GIOVANNI ANTONIO: born in Vicenza, Venetia, 1679–1746; sopranist, very fine composer, a calumniator, pupil of Pistocchi (see Pistocchi), teacher of Bologna's famous Father Martini.[54]

It is sometimes reported that he was Bernacchi's voice teacher. This is erroneous. Riccieri was only six years older than Bernacchi (see Bernacchi), and both were pupils of Pistocchi. Riccieri had such a bad temper that nobody could get along with him, not even his best disciple, the good-natured Giambattista Martini (Father Martini). Most of his compositions may be found in the unique library of Bologna's Liceo Musicale.

SENESINO (FRANCESCO BERNARDI): born in Siena, Tuscany, *ca.* 1680–1750; excellent sopranist, Handel singer, a giant. He was *not* a pupil of Bernacchi, as de Martini of the Paris conservatory in his *Histoire du chant* reports, but he preceded the latter, in 1720, as Handel singer in London, where he sang for nine years. **He was the first to use the so-called *aria di baule*.**[55]

SENESINO (ANDREA MARTINI): born in Siena, Tuscany, 1761–1819; sopranist, a beauty. He was beloved by all for his good manners, for his righteousness and for his kindness. He never had any scandalous love affair. He was extremely cultured and was befriended by many outstanding men of his day. Canova, Cimarosa, and Asioli were among his best friends,[56] and it was his voice that inspired Cimarosa to write the previously quoted, famous little poem "*La tua voce soave, . . .*"

SENESINO (FERDINANDO TENDUCCI): born in Siena, Tuscany, *ca.* 1736-after 1800; sopranist, composer, Handel singer, Handel conductor, teacher. The beauty of his voice did not last long. He scandalized the public in 1767, when he married

---

[54] See Part II, footnote 16, p. 43.

[55] See this Part, footnote 45, p. 115.

[56] Bonifazio Asioli (1769–1832) was a good theoretician, a composer and an instrumentalist. As a teacher he was so greatly appreciated that he was chosen on Haydn's recommendation to instruct Mozart's son Charles. It proved to be a thankless mission because Charles' life achievement consisted in a clerk's job in a government that did not want Mozart's son to starve. Asioli was nominated in 1808 the first teacher of counterpoint at the newly founded conservatory of Milan, and it was for this school that he wrote *Principe elementari di musica,* G. Ricordi, which is still in use and has been translated into English.

For the biography of Cimarosa see this Part, footnote 29, p. 102.

Antonio Canova (1757–1822) was the famous Italian sculptor of *Amor and Psyche* (Louvre, Paris), of *Perseus with the Head of Medusa* (Vatican), of *Napoleon I* (Brera Palace, Milan), of *The Three Graces* (Leningrad), and so forth.

one of his pupils, the sixteen year old Dorothy Maunsell, but the marriage was annulled by decree in 1775.

He wrote for English voice students *Instructions of Mr. Tenducci to his Scholars,* London, about 1785, published by Longman and Broderip. These contain vocal exercises plus twenty-one short rules on singing on the first page. The ninth rule outlines Aristotle's and Bel Canto's important law regarding the unification of the registers. It is the only published, explicit document on this topic written by an Italian vocal virtuoso of the eighteenth century. I quote this precious gem in its original wording and style:

> "IX Never to force the Voice, in order to extend its Compass in the VOCE DI PETTO upwards; but rather to cultivate the VOCE DI TESTA in what is called FALSETTO, in order to join it well and imperceptibly, to the VOCE DI PETTO for fear of incurring the disagreeable Habit of singing in the Throat, or through the Nose;—unpardonable Faults in a Singer."

Such unification is treated elaborately in Part I of this manual (p. 14).

Bernardi, Martini, and Tenducci are not Christian, but family names. Thus, obviously, the three Senesinos were by no means members of one and the same family. They were gifted poor boys of Siena who had taken their names from their native town, because the latter had paid for their castration and munificent education.

TOSI, PIER FRANCESCO (*Don*): born in Cesena, Emilia, *ca.* 1656–after April 1732 in Faenza, Italy, and not in 1727 in London; contraltist, composer, diplomatist in the service of the Austrian court, priest, knighted, famous teacher, very kind.

Pier Francesco studied with his father Giuseppe Felice, who was an organist, a composer and one of the charter members of Bologna's Philharmonic Academy. Pier Francesco was castrated when he was extremely young. He sang with much success in Italy and throughout Europe, but was always unhappy. When he was only twenty-six years of age he established himself as a teacher in London (1682), where he also gave many concerts and was highly honored by the English aristocracy. From 1705–1711 he was in the service of the Austrian court, not only as one of its teachers and artists but also as a secret diplomatic agent. Evidently he was a better artist than diplomat, because in the latter role he suffered much hardship while on a secret mission to the Republic of Genoa in 1706/7. He even lost, for a short period, the good graces of his patron, Emperor Joseph I (1705–1711),[57] who had sent him to Genoa, and whose interests he had

---

[57] Joseph I is often referred to as the founder of Vienna's Academy of Fine Arts (Akademie der Bildenden Künste). But this famous institution was founded in 1692, thus, obviously, under Leopold I, and when Joseph, born in 1678, was only fourteen years of age. See also this Part, The *Musici,* Orsini, p. 117.

attempted to serve there to the best of his abilities—a poor lark, choked by calumnies and intrigues.

Tosi's chief contribution to vocal art and culture is his treatise *Opinioni de' cantori antichi e moderni,* Bologna, 1723, only posthumously translated into English by the composer Jean Ernest Galliard[58] and printed by J. Wilcox under the title *Observations on the florid song, etc.,* London, 1742. The latter was re-edited twice, first in Brussels in 1743 and then again in London in 1906. This famous book treats of and explains many fundamental laws of the old Italian school.

If today's voice teachers would endeavor to read the first chapter, headed *Osservazioni,* in the original form of the year 1723, avoiding any personal interpretation, if they would read and reread these eleven brief but precious pages until they have fully absorbed each single sentence, we surely would have a higher average standard of singing.

VELLUTI, Giovanni Battista: born in Pausula near Ancona, the Marches, 1780–1861; excellent as sopranist, as actor, and as musician; very handsome, knighted; **the last *musico* who was an opera singer.**

He made his debut when he was twenty, toured throughout all Europe, and was applauded and honored for his most musical and expressive singing. His voice, somewhat lacking in the high notes, was velvety in the middle range. When Napoleon I heard him at Milan, he said: "One has to be not entirely a man to sing like this"; in 1812 Vienna struck medals of him and celebrated him in poems. Velluti's echo notes[59] were famous; wherever he sang, people came from afar to hear this echo.

When he sang at the Scala of Milan in May, 1814, it was not only his last appearance in this center of music but also the last time for any *musico* to fill this opera house with his captivating and enchanting voice.

Rossini wrote for him *Aureliano in Palmira.* This opera was given at the Scala of Milan, in 1813, and turned out an utter failure, for which Rossini very unjustly blamed Velluti.

Meyerbeer wrote for him *Il crociato in Egitto.* This work had its first performance at the theater Fenice of Venice, in 1824, and in it Meyerbeer[60] developed

---

[58] Jean Ernest Galliard (1687–1749) studied in Hanover (Germany) with the French composer Jean Baptiste Farinelli (1655–*ca.* 1720). Grove reports that Jean Baptiste Farinelli was an uncle of "the singer Farinelli." This represents a rather ridiculous statement for a first-class dictionary of musicians. See this Part, Farinelli, p. 109.

[59] Singers and voice teachers interested in the production of echo notes will find them treated in Part II, Chapter I:A: §2. VI. d) *Suoni Filati a Flauto* or Echo Notes, p. 65.

[60] Giacomo Meyerbeer (1791–1864) was born in Berlin, the son of a very rich banker, and received an excellent education. He died in Paris, but was buried in Berlin. Much literature exists concerning this great composer, whose roots lay deep in Bel Canto and whose first five operas were strongly influenced by Rossini. Therefore, I will limit myself to reminding the reader of the masterpieces he wrote after *Il crociato in Egitto,* wherein

for the first time his famous personal style. It was an enormous success for both, composer and singer.

Velluti came to London only in 1825. London's society had heard no *musico* for a long time and was very excited. There were two parties. One was craving to hear again "one God, one Farinelli" (see Farinelli); the other showed open animosity toward Velluti even before he had sung. Although very disillusioned, he won and was re-engaged; but the second season, the ever-growing English animosity against his status handicapped this big and sincere artist, and he was never at his best. When he left, it was a sad departure from a land he loved.

Handsome Velluti, who was very lucky in love, was proud and shy. He suffered greatly from the endless humiliations and insults he had to endure merely because of his status. They came in this new epoch even from artists as great as Mendelssohn (1809–1847), and Mendelssohn surely should have known better.

He retired early, lived as a rich man in his own majestic villa in Dolo, not far from Venice on the Brenta Riviera,[61] but was never happy. He used to say to his friends: "Thank God that I am one of the last disgraced."

Meyerbeer had found himself. They are *Robert le Diable, Les Huguenots, Le Prophète, Dinorah* and *L'Africaine,* his last and best work; they were all in the repertoire of every important opera house throughout the world before the rapid decline of vocal art that started after World War I.

[61] In some reference books the name Dolo is distorted into Delo; there is no such place near Venice.—The Brenta Riviera borders the lower part of the Brenta Canal. In its chain of parks stood a series of luxurious villas that were thought of as resorts and owned by the Venetian aristocracy of bygone times of graceful grandeur. Some are still standing. The best-known such villa is perhaps the enormous Villa Pisani, today's Villa Nationale, at Strà, with its famous fresco by Tiepolo.

Appendix

VOICE DEFECTS

Introduction

This manual attempts to explain in a brief but precise manner the style of Bel Canto with its famous virtuosities (Part II). It further presents in detailed fashion the vocal technique (Part I) which will enable the future artist to sing successfully the masterpieces of that incomparable style as well as our modern music.

I have not treated the defects of the voice in the manual itself. They do not belong to Bel Canto, and no defects can be acquired when one studies its technique under an able teacher. Moreover, most voice defects will disappear, whatever may have caused them. It is understood, of course, that the young student must be mentally and physically healthy.

Since it is my sincere desire to help singers rid themselves of the defects which handicap them in becoming worthy artists, I shall now explain the reasons for these defects, and what has to be done to overcome them, to the best of my ability. I hope that my readers will understand me, and will be able to free themselves of these obstacles, because *"the road of music is one of the many, on which the the soul returns to Heaven"* (Torquato Tasso, 1544–1595).

§1
Singing Out of Tune

A person sings out of tune because of his or her defective hearing or because of accidental causes. If the wrong intonation is due to defective hearing, it signifies that the mind cannot grasp the pitch of a tone. This person will never be able to sing. But the teacher must exercise great caution in judging a beginner to be tone-deaf. There are beginners who grasp a tone with great precision with their minds, but cannot produce this tone in the right pitch with their voices because their head resonances are completely out of balance with the voice producer.[1] They are mostly timid introverts and therefore should be handled lovingly and with the greatest patience or they will develop an inferiority complex that might handicap them for the rest of their lives, and this not merely in singing. Such beginners need only to be set on the right track, in order to stop singing off pitch.

If parents would take just as good care of their baby's ear training as they do of their baby's food, this problem would present itself less often. A person who as a little baby has been cradled into slumber by lullabies hummed in perfect pitch, and in infancy has been cheered by a mother's singing full of harmony and

---

[1] See also this Appendix, §2.b) Guttural Voice, p. 130 and §4. The Shaky Voice, p. 132.

beauty, will not sing off pitch. Our babyhood and our childhood are of the utmost importance for our development in life. For instance: how can a child who has to practice on a piano out of tune develop a perfect sense for pitch? If a strong sense for pitch is inborn, the nervous system of such a sensitive child will suffer greatly in consequence, and the child may grow into a tense and difficult adult. If the child's sense for pitch is not naturally strong, this sense not only cannot develop but its rudiments, supplied by nature, will be slowly destroyed. American and British youngsters are the best-fed and the best-dressed children on earth. Their parents willingly buy them expensive toys, but "for a young child *any* instrument, *any* music teacher will do." Instead, the first teacher of violin or the first teacher of piano has a far-reaching influence on a child's mind—and this for good and for bad. In an era when most children are sent to nursery schools, the young teachers there should have well-placed speaking voices and should always be capable of singing in pitch the nursery rhymes they teach. Yet in fact they sing them usually more or less off pitch. This is very harmful for the little ones, especially if at home they hear no singing, or *worse,* nothing but faulty singing. It would be wise for such parents to give their baby the best-trained canary they are able to find as its first pet. The canary will awaken the baby each dawn with a flood of well-timbered scales and trilled love songs in perfect pitch. Besides, nursery schools should be obliged to play recordings of classical music at least once each school day. These recordings should be the finest procurable, not haphazard discards. The very same recordings should be repeated and repeated during playtime, so that the young hearing may be molded and educated "without any strain." The sense for tone purity, the feeling for harmony of the average child would be greatly improved. To teach the progenies of generations whose ears have been awakened in early childhood—what satisfaction for the music teachers of the future! Let us return to the singers of our generation.

For the most part it may be said that singers, male and female, who force their voices tend to sharp when ascending, while when descending, being never masters of their breath, they tend to flat. Therefore they sound out of tune, and this is due to their very bad technique and to their uneducated, rather than faulty ear.

In addition to this, many women have difficulty in the intonation of the interval of a descending fourth between the head and the falsetto register,[2] because they do not know how to handle the latter. As soon as the middle range of their voices are placed **securely** above the breath, this phenomenon disappears.

A similar thing often happens to men. Only, instead of the descending fourth, they have difficulty with the interval of an ascending sixth, between the chest and the falsetto register.[2] The harder they try the more off pitch they sing this interval, without understanding the real cause, which is that they are only able either to shout with clumsy chest voices, or to use an empty falsetto (which means a falsetto that is not anchored in the chest). They ignore the flexibility and the powerful beauty

---

[2] See Part I, §6, I. The Registers and Their Union, p. 14, and check most carefully on its Fig. 6—Table of Registers, p. 15.

of the mixed voice—ignore completely Caruso's enchanting *voix mixte*. Thus, such offensive singing out of tune is not due to an innate defect of the ear, *it is due to ignorance*.

Almost all light sopranos with a bad voice production are incapable of singing correctly chromatic scales, and therefore are terrified of them. Even in such cases generally the ear is not at fault, since after the emission has been rectified nearly all of them overcome their former difficulty with the chromatic scales, especially if they have been taught to hear the difference between a major and a minor semitone.[3]

Most women flat their top notes at the beginning of their menstruation.[4] This is one of the reasons why, if possible, they should avoid singing in public or making important auditions during this period. They will never be at their best at that time.

The voices of all pregnant women tend to become more or less flat after the fifth month. They should not sing in public. Also, they should avoid singing their high notes and should never train when tired. Yet, by no means should they neglect to keep the middle range flexible and in good shape.

Most voices, and all tenors and sopranos, flat in the high range if the singers "live" too strenuously.[5] By the way, such voices will not merely sound flat on the top notes but also throughout all their range will sound empty, old.

All notes belonging to the falsetto register, consequently the high notes of the male voice and the notes of the middle range of the female voice, may fall off slightly from perfect pitch if the artist is tired or feels weak for some reason. We hear it happen to the most famous artists. It is a very disappointing occurrence, but it is an incident—and nothing more.

§2
Defective Timbres

a) **NASAL VOICE:** A voice is nasal when it partly resounds in the nose itself, a condition which may be brought about for different reasons.

ANATOMIC ANOMALIS of the nasal cavities or the nasal septum; obstructions in the nose, such as vegetations, tumors, polyps, etc.: For these, only the physician can be of help.

CORYZA: The disturbing snuffling (nasalization) of the voice will disappear with the clearing of the coryza (cold in the head).

WEAK NASAL MUSCLES: These can and should be strengthened little by little by

---

[3] See also Part II, Chapter I: A: §2. II. The Semitones and the Chromatic Scales, p. 41.

[4] See also the following page, §2.c) Harsh Voice, and §3. FOR WOMEN, p. 132.

[5] See Part I, §3. The Voice, last para.: It may be mentioned here . . . , p. 8.

the following exercises. Stand erect but without tension; draw in the part of the abdomen below the navel, as well as the navel itself; alternately widen and relax the nostrils without breathing, and keep all other muscles of the face motionless. One should practice this first after having exhaled, because it will be easier, then after having inhaled. After having mastered this movement, open the nostrils and keep them wide open as long as possible without breathing or without even letting the slightest amount of air escape while all other muscles of the face are relaxed and motionless. As soon as one is able to do this exercise, one should start to keep the nostrils wide open while breathing exclusively through the nose with the mouth shut in a most supple smile; both inhalation and exhalation should be extremely short and rapid, and, nevertheless, always silent; the breath must not even lightly touch the nasal passages. The summary of all this is: learn to keep the nasal passages wide open and free at all times.

Simultaneously the student should learn to attack and sing above the breath, as explained in Part I of the treatise. It will be hard on him in the beginning, but with serious persistence he cannot fail to overcome all nasal singing and speaking.

b) **GUTTURAL VOICE:** A voice is guttural (throaty) when it is choked in the throat or, to put it another way, when the sound waves are obstructed during the sound production.

The organs that by their incorrect movements and contractions can render a voice guttural are, principally, the tongue and, in relation to the latter, the larynx, the soft palate, the contractile parts of the pharynx, and, of course, the epiglottis. The throat muscles of such persons are often very weak, and so is the soft palate. They are *always* untrained in keeping the throat open in its posterior part, and, naturally, the opening of the throat is more or less out of balance with the resonances.

A voice produced in a wide open and free throat will never sound throaty (guttural), because the sound waves will not be obstructed during sound production. Such a free and rich voice may be acquired by controlling the emission in the manner I have explained and elaborated most scrupulously in Part I of this treatise.

To correct a guttural voice is a most nerve-racking task for the teacher, especially if the voice is also nasal. It can be accomplished successfully only if both teacher and student are persistent. The teacher must be patient and conscientious, must have a free throat, and must know his business thoroughly; the student must be patient, and must assiduously strive always to **speak**—exactly in the manner in which he is "supposed" to sing—**with his voice above his breath, else he never will be able to overcome this vocal handicap.**

c) **HARSH VOICE:** A voice can be harsh due either to bad emission or to some physical reason, such as hypertrophy of the tonsillary glands, fatigue during menstruation in very young women,[6] colds, or excessive use of tobacco. The better the voice is placed, the less chance there is of its becoming harsh.

---

[6] See also the foregoing page, §1. Singing out of Tune, Most women flat . . . , and §3. FOR WOMEN, p. 132.

d) **HOOTING VOICE** (*Voce Tubata*): A hooting voice is **never an innate defect;** it is a defect of training. The hooting voice, which is heard so often, produces in the listener the sensation of hearing sounds pouring forth from a tube, reminding him of locomotive whistles or of our air raid sirens, or as some folks put it . . . "the wailful sough of the winter wind" or "the howling of a sick dog." The Italians have very insulting standard names for such offenders for whom they know no compassion. They call the men *cane* [male dog], the women *cagna* [female dog] or *gatta* [she-cat]. All hooting is due to a continual darkening of the voice in such manner as to result in the almost complete shutting off of the head resonances and the forming of one long tube out of the pharynx and the mouth cavity.[7] This happens if the teacher confuses the resonances of the head with the resonances of the mouth, volume with intensity,[8] dark with round. Owing to such ignorance, the teacher will, with endless exercises on $ó(5)$ and $u = oo(7)$,[9] darken the voice of his pupil in order to enlarge and beautify it. He does not understand that his pupil's voice, because stripped of its metal, will be without clarity, without sweetness, without charm—in fact, it will be mere whistles and howls.

In the body of this treatise—in Part I, §6. II. The Timbre of the Voice— the reader will find explained how one should study in order to overcome this defect.

e) **SHRILL VOICE** (*Voce Pettegola, Voce Stridula*), also called white voice (*voce bianca*): A voice can be shrill naturally, or this defect can be due to a basic vocal training on $i(1)$.[9]

Shrillness is more or less a defect of Latin voices. Native English-speakers need have no fear of this. It is generally the light sopranos and light tenors of Latin countries trained in some inferior school that have white, shrill voices. It is necessary to round out—**not to darken!**—such tight and crude voices, without, however, their losing any of their characteristic agility and carrying quality. Then their range, so often small, will rapidly increase, and their timbre should become beautiful in its subsequent development. But, it is not an easy task—far from it.

§3

The Veiled Voice

A voice is veiled when the air emitted from the lungs is not entirely used in phonation, in musical and speech sound production.[10] Such leakage (*coulage*)

---

[7] A voice may be darkened for expression when the composition calls for such an interpretation. Exercises should never be darkened! See Part II, Chapter II: §3. The Application of Various Timbres, p. 87.

[8] See also this Appendix, §5. The Weak Voice, p. 134.

[9] See Part I, §10. The Study of Vowels and Diphthongs and Their Application to English Singing, p. 25.

[10] See Part I, §5. Sound Attack, p. 12.

comes about if the contraction of the vocal cords is not perfect, especially at the extreme ends, and is due either to some pathological reason or to bad habit in the sound attack.[11] In the first case, the singer should stop singing and consult a good laryngologist. In the second case, the voice will lose its "veil" when the vocal cords are trained to contract in the correct manner. This result will be attained by attending with great patience to the attack of sound above the breath (the preparatory act or effort),[10] and, later, by having the pupil do considerable work with the shut voice.[12]

It is very important to be able to distinguish whether the veiled voice is caused by defective functioning of the vocal cords due to bad habits, or whether it is caused by some pathological defect, since **in the latter case any vocal exercise would be injurious.** But a really good teacher can tell which is the reason for the veil.

FOR WOMEN: There are sensitive female voices that cannot contract the vocal cords in a perfect manner during menstruation,[13] or even some time before. As a result their voices will be veiled, especially in the medium register

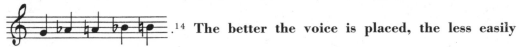

.[14] **The better the voice is placed, the less easily and the less often will this come about.** But if it happens, the singer need only refrain from singing for a day or two, take a good rest, sleep as much as possible, and forget the woes of life.

§4

The Shaky Voice

A voice can be shaky (*voce tremula*) for different physiological reasons. If I say that generally the shakiness in a voice depends on the weakness of the crico-thyroid muscles,[15] *or* on a nervous weakness of the tongue, *or* on a lack of balance between the organ of phonation and the head resonances,[16] *or* on the weakness of the diaphragm, *or* on a combination of these, such division will not be of help to the average reader. Therefore, I will treat this far too often encountered voice defect very unscientifically but more practically by distinguishing between the beginner

---

[11] Even the pathological state may be the consequence of bad habits in sound attack.

[12] See Part I, §9. The Shut Voice, p. 23.

[13] See also this Appendix, §1. Singing out of Tune, Most women flat . . . , p. 129 and §2.c) Harsh Voice, p. 130.

[14] See Part I, §6. I. The Registers and Their Union, footnote 17, p. 19.

[15] The crico-thyroid muscles are situated on the exterior part of the larynx. They produce a certain tension of the vocal cords. See Part I, Fig. 2—Anterior Median Line of Neck, p. 6.

[16] See this Appendix, §1. Singing Out of Tune, p. 127 and §2,b) Guttural Voice, p. 130.

with a shaky voice; the old student with a shaky voice; and the professional artist whose voice is beginning to shake.

THE BEGINNER WITH A SHAKY VOICE often shakes with his voice merely because he does not know any better. Such a student sometimes will also have a weak voice.[17]   It suffices to teach him in the manner that I have explained in Part I of this manual. This pupil must work only within the limit of one octave, changing the exercises continually, and his teacher must take great care that the pupil's tongue is uninterruptedly in the right position.[18] After a few lessons he will no longer have a shaky voice.

In such a beginner not only the voice and the mind should be educated. He must definitely learn to have much regard for his health, since he has not only a delicate throat but most probably also nervous intestines. He should be handled with love and greatest patience![19]

THE OLD STUDENT WITH A SHAKY VOICE generally has this shakiness because he has the habit of forcing his voice. He sings or shouts for hours at a time, apparently not knowing what "singing" means. He must start by learning the most fundamental laws of the old Italian school of singing. He, too, must start all exercises within the extension of one octave only, without ever singing sustained notes, non-legato agility, and trills. Since he certainly will have the habit of attacking with a shock of the glottis, he must be trained with special care to attack in *flautato* manner above the breath.[20] While singing, he should imagine that he is swallowing each note, emitted exclusively on the vowel *a* (4),[21] until slowly, ever so slowly, the shakiness disappears. Then, and only then, can this student begin the regular study of voice emission.

This student can overcome the shakiness in his voice only, by placing himself in the hands of a very conscientious teacher, and even then, only if he is really determined to stop shouting. It will **not** be, as it is in the case of the beginner, a matter of a few lessons. Much time and patience will be needed for this unfortunate individual.

THE PROFESSIONAL ARTIST WHOSE VOICE IS BEGINNING TO SHAKE. There are artists who, at the very outset of their careers,[22] begin to develop a voice that wavers and shakes.

This happens because these singers have beautiful voices and have allowed themselves to be flattered into singing parts too heavy for their vocal organs.[23]

---

[17] See the following page, §5. The Weak Voice.

[18] **But no student should ever become aware of this care, or he surely will not overcome being handicapped by his tongue.**

[19] As a mother cradles her young.

[20] See Part I, §5. Sound Attack, p. 12.

[21] See Part I, §10. The Study of the Vowels and Diphthongs and Their Application to English Singing, p. 25.

[22] Sometimes already in the second or third year!

[23] See this Appendix, §5. The Weak Voice, the two last para., p. 135.

They can hold their own in the beginning, but as they have to repeat this "heavy stuff" day in day out, again and again, their throats cannot resist such a strain. Instead of becoming more beautiful and more perfect, their lovely voices begin to shake.

These artists will be finished before their time if they do not stop singing "with their entire capital." For them there is only one remedy. They must rest their voices completely from two to four weeks, then work eight to ten days "solely" with the shut voice.[24] When they are in true form once more, they should choose a less heavy repertory.

But if such an artist is not cured in time, he will so ruin his beautiful voice that soon there will be no remedy for him whatsoever.

§5

The Weak Voice

First of all, I would like to clear up a misconception often encountered. **Small** voices and **weak** voices are not synonymous. If a voice is "naturally small," nothing can be done to change it; and **nothing should be done to change it.** A voice can be very small (in volume) and still be a sparkling jewel (full of intensity).[25] To enlarge it would mean simply to ruin it.

A weak voice is one which lacks intensity (strength). Take heed, **intensity, not volume;** take care not to confuse intensity with volume.

A voice can be weak for three reasons: general weakness of the entire organism; natural weakness of the vocal organs; and weakness of the vocal organs due to faulty voice emission.

GENERAL WEAKNESS OF THE ENTIRE ORGANISM: A voice may be weak if the student is weak and anemic. Such a student first must strengthen his body before beginning the study of singing, otherwise he will ruin his voice forever. Also a

---

[24] See Part I, §9. The Shut Voice, p. 23.

[25] Alessandro Bonci, born in Cesana, 1870, was a student at the Academy of Music in Pesaro, the renowned Liceo Rossini, where he studied voice faithfully day by day for five years under Felice Coen (1856–1903). The singing of Bonci, who had a **very small voice,** was insinuatingly sweet; this was due entirely to the pure timbre of his voice which was most perfectly schooled, and to the finesse with which he used it. He was judged by many Italians superior to Caruso.

Sigrid Anderson, the Swedish nightingale, whose real name was Arnoldson, wife of the Viennese impresario Alfred Fischof, was born in Stockholm, 1861. She was a pupil of Maurice Strakosch (1825–1878), and of Désirée Artôt (1835–1907). This famous light soprano had an extraordinary extension. Her **very small voice,** full of spirit, was of a rare sweetness and charm, even in the notes above high $c(c^3)$. After having sung in almost every part of the globe, she opened a singing school in Vienna. At seventy-two, her little voice was still like a clear bell.

thyroid gland which is not working correctly may be the cause of said weakness. It is the duty of the teacher to insist upon his pupil consulting a physician. Only with the latter's approval should such a person study singing.

NATURAL WEAKNESS OF THE VOCAL ORGANS: If a voice is weak (*fiacca*), because the vocal organs or part of them are weak—a common occurrence in untrained very young voices—these organs will become stronger automatically while studying in the manner I have explained in the body of this treatise. But a conscientious teacher will be careful in the development of the extension of such a pupil. He must wait until the voice becomes perfectly timbred in the medium register. Only then may he proceed with the high and low notes. A good teacher will make such a voice not only stronger but also bigger—which means that volume will be acquired in addition to intensity.

WEAKNESS OF THE VOCAL ORGANS DUE TO FAULTY VOICE EMISSION: The same rules apply to this type of voice. By taking care of the emission the weakness will gradually disappear. But, if this student is past thirty, I advise him to give up hopes of a real career. He can learn to sing with perfect technique, and also with taste and with charm, but, I cannot see him ever becoming a successful artist.

Once again: weak does not mean small. **A clear, penetrating voice does not always have to be a big one!** Weakness means lack of intensity, and a clear, penetrating voice is the result of intensity of the sound.

The tiny voice of a small soprano[26] can be a silvery ringing little bell that will touch the heartstrings, but if it has to sing *Tosca* . . . then good-bye to the clear, musical tone of silver! A light tenor voice with lively sunshine in the high register[27] cannot sing a Radames (*Aïda*) without having the high notes lose their sparkle.

We often hear a lyric soprano with a clear, bell-like voice singing the part of a dramatic soprano, or a lyric tenor and sometimes even a light tenor, a tenorino, singing the heavy part of a dramatic tenor.

Intensity is often confused with volume,[28] and that is the source of much sorrow.

§6
Weak Notes

A beginner will always have one register weaker than another. It is the duty of the teacher to mold the voice so that the inequalities will disappear from all the notes of the range.

In the body of this treatise—in Part I, §6. I. The Registers and Their Union—the reader will find explained what must be done to achieve this.

---

[26] As in *Lucia di Lammermoor* (Donizetti).

[27] As in *I Puritani* (Bellini).

[28] See this Appendix, §4. The Shaky Voice: The professional artist whose voice is beginning to shake, p. 133.

§7
The Tired Voice

When the voice of an artist is tired, it does not necessarily mean that the artist himself is tired, but rather that he does not feel well. If so, he should not sing if he can avoid doing so.

The same rule holds true for the student. He positively should not sing when he does not feel well.

A singer whose throat tires easily either has a defective constitution and will not endure in his career, or he is forcing, that is to say ruining, his voice.

The vocal apparatus in a healthy youth whose entire voice is faultlessly placed above the breath in the focus of the resonances, as well as firmly anchored in the chest, will never become tired during the performance, even should the singer tire physically. But he must not abuse this gift lest he lose it.

******

I have perhaps been cruel, and, at times, impolite in this Appendix. The unpleasant truth is sometimes necessary when one sincerely wishes to help.

Index